KALARIPAYATTU

India's Own Combat Culture

G Varun Yadav

Qurate
qur atebooks.com

KALARIPAYATTU: India's Own Combat Culture
G Varun Yadav

Published in 2024

© Published by

Qurate Books Pvt. Ltd.
Goa 403523, India
www.quratebooks.com
Tel: 1800-210-6527, Email: info@quratebooks.com

ISBN: 978-93-58988-67-3

"You don't choose Kalaripayattu,
Kalaripayattu chooses you"

ABOUT THE AUTHOR

G. Varun Yadav is an engineering graduate and a dedicated researcher in the traditional martial art of Kalaripayattu. He has been practicing Kalaripayattu and other forms of combat since 2011, training under several esteemed martial arts experts. Varun is a disciple of Shri. Jawahar Gurukkal (Guruvayoor) and Shri. Ranjan Mullaratt Gurukkal (Bangalore). He has also gained knowledge of Kalam Chavitt Kalaripayattu from the renowned maestro of the style, Shri. Ashraf Gurukkal (London). Additionally, he is a practitioner in modern combat systems such as Rapid Assault Tactics and Shifu Kanishka Combatives, under the tutelage of legendary martial artist Shri. Tuhon Shifu Kanishka Sharma. In 2016, Varun earned a national-level gold medal in Pro-Amateur Muay Thai Kickboxing under the mentorship of Shri. Kru M. N. Vikram (Mysuru). Over the years, he has also explored various styles of Silambam, Grappling, and Kuthuvarisai, under the guidance of various notable teachers. Currently, he serves as the lead instructor at his martial arts institute, KALARI SADHANA: MYSURU, located in Mysuru, Karnataka.

KALARI SADHANA

MYSURU

ACKNOWLEDGEMENT

It has been a long-held dream of mine to write a simple book on Kalaripayattu that would help a layperson understand the combat system and its intricacies. As this dream becomes a reality, I wholeheartedly express my gratitude to my teacher, Shri. Jawahar Gurukkal for his knowledge and guidance. My heartfelt thanks go to Shri. Ashraf Gurukkal (London) for always being there for me. I have drawn great inspiration from my idol and mentor, the legendary martial artist Tuhon Shifu Kanishka Sharma, on how to immerse oneself in one's passion.

I am also grateful to my friends Sushanth S. P. (Bengaluru), Mahendra M.N. (Mysuru), Anudeep Hegde (Karkala), Chamind Erakkil (Guruvayoor), Sachu Shanmugan (Guruvayoor), Vishnu P. V. (Mysuru), Abhishek (Mysuru), Rajendra (Mysuru), Niharika (Mysuru), and many others who have helped me at different stages of the book publication. I also thank my family, who have always been my backbone through all walks of life. My special regards go to my maternal grandparents (Mrs. Komala Ramana and Mr. Y. Venkataramana) for all their support and affection. I seek love and blessings from heaven from my paternal grand-parents Late Shri. P. M. Doddanna and Late Shri. Nagamma (Ichanahalli, Periyapatna). Lastly, I express my gratitude to all those who belong to my martial arts family of 'Kalari Sadhana: Mysuru' for always being by my side.

FOREWORD

CHAKRAVARTHY SULIBELE

Notable Orator, Writer, Columnist and Founder of Yuva Brigade and Sodari Nivedita Pratishtana.

Who doesn't need martial arts and self-defense techniques? These skills empower us to rely on our strength rather than external dependencies. However, in a world dominated by robotics and advanced AI, the question arises: Are such arts and techniques still necessary? This book attempts to find an answer.

Many trace the roots of combat systems and self-defense techniques to Bharath, where they are estimated to have originated around 3,000 years ago. The oldest of these is Kalaripayattu. In today's relentless world, people who lack the time to stay fit often seek others for protection. This book aims to inspire readers to awaken their inner strength.

The book would not hold much significance if it only covered Kalaripayattu with some background and a few images of practitioners at the Gurukula. However, the author, Varun, delves deeper, questioning the Indian origins of Kalari, particularly its Hindu roots. It's often suggested that anything superior or excellent must have originated outside of Bharath. Aryans, considered the superior race, are said to be outsiders. The Vedas, the epitome of ancient literature, are thought to have foreign origins. Similarly, while 'Kalari' cannot be proven foreign, many have tried to distance it from the 'Hindu' domain. Yet, as the saying goes, "A gem need not be searched for; its aura draws people to it."

There is a widely held belief that South India is the birthplace of martial arts, and this is attributed to Parashurama. According to legend, the wicked king Kartavirya Arjuna killed Jamadagni after accepting his hospitality, sparking Parashurama's oath of vengeance. Parashurama not only killed Kartavirya Arjuna but also vowed to circle the world 21 times, eliminating all Kshatriyas. Empowered by intense penance, he fulfilled his vow, then, as instructed by Rishi Kashyapa, donated his conquered lands and settled in southern Bharath. There, he expanded the land by pushing back the sea and taught the art of combat. To this day, devotees believe that Lord Sadashiva imparted Dhanurveda to Parashurama.

Parashurama is believed to have begun the tradition of Kalari in Kerala. A traditional Malayalam song describes the divine origin of Kerala, the founding of 108 Kalaris, and Parashurama's instruction of 21 Gurus in the art of enemy annihilation. Today's Kerala may have changed, but history remains unchanged, doesn't it?

This book thoroughly explores the history and present state of Kalari. It also highlights the traditions that have evolved within its practice. A disciple cannot attain knowledge by merely obeying the Guru; they must also bow to the Divine. Hindu culture generously enrolls students as young as seven in Kalari Gurukula, providing them with daily instruction. It's noteworthy that martial arts in the Western world are usually associated with

China. However, there is substantial evidence that South Indian combat systems have influenced Chinese martial arts.

Aside from Kalari, learning martial arts in general can be enlightening. Numerous research papers in the West have examined the effects of martial arts on the body, mind, and intellect. Ron Roberts from Kingston University, in his paper, states that continuous practice of martial arts enables practitioners to detach themselves from immediate reactions, with patience, introspection, and calmness becoming natural traits. In some cases, teachers have noted significant improvements in behavior among middle-school students after they began martial arts training. This research encourages parents who keep their children away from such arts, believing academics are the sole priority. Hongle Song of Adamson University in the Philippines has shown through various experiments that students in higher education who practice martial arts tend to excel academically as well. When the mind is calm, academic improvement naturally follows.

There is no doubt that Kalaripayattu emphasizes physical control and places equal importance on mental stability. Patanjali's Ashtanga Yoga outlines various samadhi stages, and Kalaripayattu seeks to achieve similar states through its own methods. Kalaripayattu is not solely an external martial art; it is, at its core, a continuation of the Indian spiritual tradition. My friend Varun has thoroughly detailed these aspects in his work. He isn't writing about Kalaripayattu as an outsider; having practiced it at the Gurukula for many years, he shares its essence with society. He has brought the spiritual philosophy behind Kalaripayattu to light. This book, therefore, inspires both those who wish to understand Kalaripayattu and those who practice it. On behalf of society, I thank Varun for his efforts.

May this work encompass us all.

Vande,

Chakravarthy

CONTENTS

1

INTRODUCTION

Kalaripayattu is India's indigenous martial tradition, a unique blend of self-defense and healing. It amalgamates physical, psychological, and spiritual practices to elevate human consciousness to higher states for holistic well-being.

Kalaripayattu is a combination of two words: Kalari and Payattu. Kalari means place of practice or gymnasium, and Payattu means to practice anything related to warfare. Kalari can be broken down into "Kala + Ari," where Kala refers to weeds, and Ari is to kill. So, Kalari is to kill the weeds in you, both physical and psychological.

2

HISTORICAL BACKGROUND

According to popular belief, Northern-style Kalaripayattu (Chapter 3) was formulated by Warrior Sage Parashurama, who happens to be Lord Vishnu's sixth Avatar.

It is said that Parashurama revived Parashurama Kshetra, which is present-day Kerala and part of coastal Karnataka from the Arabian Sea. He established 108 Kalaris and trained 21 of his disciples in Kalaripayattu.

Figure: *Sage Parashurama*

Figure: *Sage Agasthya*

Another legend states that the Immortal Sage Agasthya, who is said to be a maestro in martial arts and medicine, is the Guru of the Southern style of Kalaripayattu (Chapter 3) and the Tamil lineage of martial arts like Silambam, Varmakalai, and Kuthuvarisai.

PARASHURAMA KSHETRA

MAP NOT TO SCALE

Figure: *Kalaripayattu has its roots in the present-day Indian states of Karnataka, Kerala and Tamil Nadu*

Sangam Literature (6th century BC—4th century AD) mentions warfare and how warriors of the Sangam era were trained in military science.

Vadakkan Pathugal (Northern Ballads of Kerala) mentions the martial arts of that age and praises legendary Kalaripayattu heroes like Aromal Chekavar, Tacholi Ottenan, and the famous female warrior Unniyarcha.

Kalaripayattu is said to have experienced its golden phase during the 12th and 13th centuries. The present-day states of Kerala, Karnataka, and Tamil Nadu were divided into small principalities, and each principality maintained its army trained in martial skills.

Although Kalaripayattu warriors were mainly from the noble Nayar caste in Northern Kerala and the Nadar caste in the Southern confluence of Tamil Nadu and Kerala, students of all castes were accepted to get training in Kalaripayattu along with primary education.

There are no gender differences in the learning and practice of Kalaripayattu, both in contemporary times and historically.

The decline of Kalaripayattu started around the 17th century due to European invasions and the introduction of firearms (guns and cannons), which began to overshadow the use of traditional weaponry.

The British banned Kalaripayattu in 1804 to respond to the Cotiote War (Kottayathu War), a strong rebellion against British rule in Kerala led by the Keralite King Kerala Varma Pazhassi Raja. His exemplary guerrilla warfare tactic posed a significant threat to the British Raj. His revolt for independence is said to have been one of the hardest for the British East India Company to counter. Realizing the resistance that Kalaripayattu warriors could pose, the British banned the practice of Kalaripayattu after the death of Pazhassi Raja.

But Kalaripayattu was kept alive in secrecy, thanks to masters who practiced and preserved it for future generations.

3

STYLES OF KALARIPAYATTU

Geographically, Kalaripayattu is divided into three distinct styles:

- Vadakkan Kalaripayattu (Northern style of Kalaripayattu)
- Thekkan Kalaripayattu (Southern style of Kalaripayattu)
- Madhyan Kalaripayattu (Central style of Kalaripayattu)

I. Sampradayams or Lineages

Despite recent geographical divisions, Kalaripayattu still works on the lines of different Sampradayams or lineages.

Aarappukai, Vattenthirippu, Odimurisseri, Dronamballi, Vallabhatta, Kalam Chavittu, Pillatangi, Adi Mura 64, and Thulunadan are a few among many sampradayams across Kerala.

Vattenthirippu is a style practiced in northern most parts of Kerala. This is a style that consists of fast, circular, and spiraling movements with various jumps. Vattam means circle, and the movements of this style are based on the shape of a circle.

Arappukai is practiced in regions in and around Kannur, i.e., to the south of the northern part of Kerala. Arappu means divisions. Lessons of this style are designed in a step-by-step manner, enabling the practitioner to practice longer sequences after mastering the smaller steps.

Pillatangi is practiced mainly near Vadakara and the Kadathanadan region of Kerala. The style of Pillatangi imitates the movements of a person carrying a baby. The word Pilla means baby. Another uniqueness of this style is that it employs diaphragmatic breathing.

Styles of Vallabhatta and Odimurisseri are practiced in the central part of Kerala.

The southern part of Kerala has a martial tradition called Adithada, influenced by Tamil martial arts.

II. Understanding the Fundamental Differences in the Geographical Bifurcation of Kalari Styles

The Northern style, attributed to Lord Parashurama, practices the system of 64 kula marmas and Ayurveda. The Southern style (related to Tamil martial arts), was created by Sage Agasthya, practices the system of 108 marmas, emphasizing Siddha medicine. The Central style has a distinctive sampradayam called Kalam Chavitt, which focuses on floor patterns and footwork. This style is mainly connected to the native and tribal communities of the region. They have their own native methods of healing and interpretation of marmas.

4

STAGES OF TRAINING

Training in Kalaripayattu is divided into four stages:

1. Meithari (body-conditioning exercises)
2. Kolthari (practice of wooden weapons)
3. Ankathari (practice of metal weapons)
4. Verumkai (barehanded techniques)

Let's look into each stage below.

1) Meithari (body-conditioning exercises)

Meithari (Chapter 12) is the initial stage, which involves sets of body-control exercises, including Vadivus (postures) and its Prayogams (applications), Chuvadu (footwork), and Kaalugal (leg raises).

Later, these fundamentals are combined to form complex sequences like Kaikuthipayatt, Meipayattu, and various Chuvadu Murai, which lead to increased mind-body coordination, agility, focus, flexibility, and stamina.

2) Kolthari (practice of wooden weapons)

Once students become physically competent, they are introduced to fighting with wooden weapons (Chapter 13).

Firstly, they are introduced to Vadi Veeshal (stick rotation) to gain control over the weapon and then to long-staff fighting (Kettukari Payattu/Neduvadi Payattu/Shareera Vadi Payattu).

Then, they are introduced to close-range wooden weapons like Cheruvadi (short stick) and Otta (curved stick), where they will be taught various attacking and blocking techniques accompanied by several weapon disarms and locks.

3) Ankathari (practice of metal weapons)

Once the students become well-versed in all the wooden weapons, they train with metal weapons (Chapter 14), which, due to their lethal nature, demand superior concentration, mind-body coordination, and agility. The metal weapons taught are the Kattaram (dagger), Udaval (fencing sword), Valum Parichayum (sword and shield), Kuntham (spear), and Urumi (flexible double-edged blade).

4) Verumkai (barehanded techniques)

Once the students have mastered all the weapons, they are taught to defend themselves with barehanded techniques (Chapter 15) against both armed and unarmed attacks. The practice here mainly involves offensive locks, counter-offensive unlocks, throws, weapon disarms, and attacking vital points (Marmas).

All these four stages are interlinked; no stage stands independent of another, and every stage is equally important.

The Guru and his lineage ultimately decide the number of adavus (lessons) and the way of practice.

Kalaris may abandon this orthodox methodology and adopt their own principles to teach their student.

5

QUALITIES OF A KALARI STUDENT

Kaka Chestham

Bako Dhyani

Swana Nidra Thadaivacha

Alpahari Grihatyagi

Bhramachari

Kalari Vidyarthi Lakshanam.

Vidhyarthi means the one who desires knowledge. Students who practice Kalari should possess these six characteristic features and qualities:

Kaka Chestham: Efforts of a crow - childhood story of persistent effort by a thirsty crow to get water which was at the bottom of the pitcher by putting pebbles into it.

Bako Dhyani: Focus of a crane - Cranes stand still in the water with a single pointed focus until they catch a big fish, letting the smaller ones pass by.

Shwana Nidra: Alertness of a dog.

Alpahaari: Giving less food to the stomach and the senses- Feeding your senses only with things that are of utmost necessity to gain knowledge.

Griha Tyagi: To leave the home (comfort zone) to stay with the Guru and learn.

Brahmachari: To follow the necessary celibacy rules until marriage.

6

TYPES OF KALARI

Kalari (the place of practice) is considered as a temple. Its consecration follows the divine principles of Vastu Shastra.

After choosing an appropriate place, the construction of a Kalari is started on an auspicious day at a Subha Muhurtham (the auspicious time of the day as per the Hindu unit of measurement of time).

Figure: *A look into Kalari Gurukulam, Thozhiyoor*

Different types of Kalaris that can be observed are:

1) Kuzhi Kalari

Generally measuring 42 (east-west direction) × 21 (north-south direction) feet, it is mainly used by martial practitioners for regular training and practice. Here, the mud is dug out about three to four feet below the ground level, and the thatched roof is made of coconut and bamboo leaves. The pit's ground is red sand mixed with various herbs that have medicinal value.

2) Anga Kalari

It measures 52 × 26 feet. It is generally used for conducting angam or competitions.

3) Taravattu Kalari

It measures around 32 × 16 feet. In ancient times, it was meant for the practice of family members of the warrior class.

4) Kurum Kalari

It was used for guerilla training.

5) Ceru Kalari

It was used for (medical) treatment (Kalari Chikitsa).

6) Kodum Kalari

A Kalari where dhyana, upasana, and meditation are practiced.

7

RITUALS OF KALARI

Kalaripayattu is not just about physical fighting, it is a lifestyle and culture that aims to make the practitioner realize one's true Self through combat training.

So, in this process, Kalari and all its physical training include rituals to discipline the student.

Upon entering the Kalari to begin training, the students must salute the ground and then the Poothara (Chapter 8), Guruthara, and Devathara trio (Chapter 9). The students then

Figure: *A student taking blessings of the Guru before starting practice*

Figure: *Shri. Jawahar Gurukkal of Kalari Gurukulam, Thozhiyoor, is performing puja on the auspicious occasion of Ayudhapooja.*

touch the Guru's feet to begin the session. A student's progress in Kalaripayattu requires a lot of discipline, dedication, and a sacred relationship with the master (Chapter 19).

In many Kalaris, chanting mantras is an essential and integral part of kalari training.

Each Vadivu (Chapter 12) is assigned a particular beej mantra. The master keeps some mantras a closely guarded secret and only shares them with the most trustworthy students for their spiritual advancement.

The Guru, or the master, leads the prayers, salutations, and meditation, guiding his disciples.

Students are initiated into newer lessons or weapon training on special days like Vijayadashami.

On the occasion, the teacher blesses the student and prays to the lineage of Guru Parampara to safeguard the student in practice and life.

8

POOTHARA

Poothara is a sacred structure located at the southwestern corner of the training Kalari. It is an upward-tapering structure with unique rituals and is believed to represent Goddess Bhadrakali. In some Kalaris, Poothara has seven tiers, which represent the seven Chakras or energy centers in the human body - namely, Sahasrara, Ajna, Vishuddhi, Anahata, Manipuraka, Swadishtana, and Muladhara. Few Kalaris adopt five steps representing the five elements or the five human senses.

Figure: *Poothara, Devathara, and Guruthara*

Some Kalaris have nine-step Pootharas, denoting Navadwara (nine gates) in the human body. Next to Poothara are two small structures, Ganapathy Thara (Deva-thara) and Guruthara, paying homage to the Hindu god Ganapathy and the lineage of Gurus. In a few lineages, the Poothara, Devathara, and Guruthara trio are worshipped as Hindu God Shiva or as Serpent deities. Every Kalari session starts and ends with the students offering a salutation to the Poothara and the Guru.

9

SALUTATIONS IN KALARIPAYATTU

Kalaripayattu across lineages have different salutations based on their beliefs and rituals.

A few salutations seen across various Kalaris are:

1. *Poothara vanakkam* (salutation to the Poothara)
2. *Kalari vanakkam* (salutation to the Kalari)
3. *Guru vanakkam* (salutation to the teacher)
4. *Ishvara vanakkam* (salutation to God)
5. *Naga vanakkam* (salutation to the snake deity)
6. *Dik vanakkam* (salutation to the directions)
7. *Ayudha vanakkam* (salutation to the Kalari weapons)
8. *Surya–Chandra vanakkam* (salutation to the sun and the moon)

Figure: *V V Shriram of Bengaluru demonstrating a salutation pose in Kalari Vanakkam*

10

KALARIPAYATTU PRAYERS

Mantra meditation and prayers are a vital and essential part of regular Kalari practice in many lineages.

Prayer recited at the beginning and ending of each class used in the Author's lineage is:

Vigneshwara
Chandika
Vishnu
Vadukischa
Tadaaguru
Kali
Vaakasthapurushu
Sapthedey Paradevatha
Namasthubhyam Namaha

This prayer represents the seven presiding deities of the Kalari and is also linked to the seven steps of the Poothara.

It also denotes the seven qualities a Kalaripayattu practitioner should attain through regular practice.

Vigneshwara represents strength and initiating power.

Chandika stands for patience and Bhumi Shakti (earth power).

Figure: *Students reciting the Kalari prayer before the beginning of the class*

Vishnu denotes Agni Shakti and commanding power.

Vadukishcha stands for lightening and Ayudhaprabhashakti (energy created when a weapon is wielded in full vigor and strength).

Tadaaguru denotes the lineage of Gurus and Guru Shakti.

Kali stands for fury and the Raudra aspect that one should possess within.

Vaakasthapurushu represents commanding power and also the sounds that can be used in combat to terrify the opponent.

Sapthedey is the seven steps of Poothara, and *Paradevatha* is one all-encompassing energy that is omnipresent, omnipotent, and omniscient.

Namastubhyam Namaha is a phrase that translates to salutations or devotional surrender of the practitioner to the above mentioned energy forms.

11

VAAYTHARI: ORAL COMMANDS

When practicing Kalari, the students make their moves according to the rhythmic oral commands of the gurukkal. These oral commands are called Vaaythari.

These are Kalari-specific technical phrases that only convey a little to non-practitioners of Kalaripayattu.

Vaaythari helps the student to have a fluid and continuous flow of movements.

Vaaytharis are mainly understood through demonstration and training under a seasoned master, as many terms don't have a uniform interpretation in the practice community.

A few styles or lineages have forms that don't carry any specific Vaaythari.

12

MEITHARI: BODY-CONDITIONING EXERCISES

I. Vadivus

Vadivus are stances or postures that a practitioner adopts during combat. They are dynamic and transitional in nature.

Vadivus are largely inspired by animals, with their offensive and defensive movements, as well as behavioral traits, carefully observed and incorporated. In some lineages, Vadivus also take inspiration from Indian Puranas or are drawn from the elements of the natural environment.

Vadivus, accompanied by the correct Chuvadu (footwork), enables Kalari practitioners to defend themselves when the situation arises.

Irrespective of the lineage, Vadivus play an essential role in the practice of Kalari.

A few of the common Vadivus practiced are:

1. Gaja (Elephant)
2. Simha (Lion)
3. Marjara (Cat)
4. Mayura (Peacock)
5. Matsya (Fish)

6. Sarpa (Snake)
7. Kukkuda (Rooster)
8. Aswa/Haya (Horse)
9. Vanara (Humanoid Apes)
10. Varaha (Wild boar)
11. Garuda (Eagle)
12. Nataraja (Lord Shiva)

The lineage of the Author adopts the concept of Ashtavadivu (8 basic postures):

Varaha

Gaja

Marjara

Simham

Sarpam

Kukkuda

Mayura

Hayamithyadi

Vadivettum

Narambuje.

Figure: *A variation of Gaja vadivu (Elephant)*

Figure: *A variation of Aswa vadivu (Horse)*

Figure*: A variation of Simha Vadivu (Lion)*

Figure: *A variation of Marjara vadivu (Cat)*

Figure: *A variation of Varaha vadivu (Wild boar)*

Figure: *A variation of Sarpa vadivu (Snake)*

Figure: *A variation of Mayura vadivu (Peacock)*

Figure: *A variation of Kukkuda vadivu (Rooster)*

In a few lineages, *Matsya* replaces *Mayura*. Some lineages follow lesser-known Vadivus, like *Ajjam* (Goat), *Shasha* (Rabbit), and *Kurma* (Tortoise).

Vadivus provide a lot of subtle inferences for a practitioner to adopt:

Elephant: Physical Strength, Groundedness and Proper Intellect.

Peacock: Psycho-Physical Balance and using the whole body by spreading various limbs to keep opponents at bay.

Rooster: Proper Gaze and Simultaneous use of limbs during combat.

Horse: Using Core Strength and Self awareness.

Wild Boar: Elbow Strikes and always having a guard to protect oneself.

Fish: Slippery nature during combat. It is also a symbol of preservation and protection in Hindu puranas.

Lion: Majestic attitude, fearlessness and righteous anger.

Snake: Precision to hit pressure points and the ability to turn in any direction with ease. It also represents Kundalini Shakti.

Few masters and lineages connect Vadivus to mantra and tantra sadhana.

Each Vadivu is said to have an associated mantra for recitation and spiritual sadhana.

For example,

Elephant: Ganapathy beej mantra

Wild boar: Varahamurthi mantra (Avatar of Lord Vishnu)

Horse: Aswarudha mantra

Peacock: Subramanya beej mantra

Lion: Narasimha mantra

Knowing and understanding the inner nuances of Vadivus will help the student experience psychological and physical upliftment.

II. Kaalugal

Kaalugal, often called leg raises in Kalaripayattu, is practiced to gain balance, proper body posture, single-pointed focus, stability, and lower body strength.

Basic Kaalugal aids the practitioner in building a proper base, physically and psychologically, for more advanced movements in the later stages.

Kaalugal, when practiced regularly, gives the student excellent hip flexibility and endurance.

Figure: *Ner Kaal (straight leg raise)*

A few common leg raises practiced in almost all Kalaris are:

1. *Ner kaal*: Straight leg raise
2. *Kon kaal*: Diagonal leg raise
3. *Veethu kaal*: Circular leg raise
4. *Iruthi kaal*: Leg raises and sit
5. *Tiruchhi kaal*: To and fro leg raise
6. *Nere Kon Veethu*: Combination of leg raise
7. *Agam kaal*: Inward leg raise
8. *Sooji kaal*: Leg raise and splits

After mastering the fundamental ones, the complexity of the leg raises increases with jumping and twisting kicks, which demands excellent mind-body coordination, physical prowess, and overall body strength.

Figure: *Iruthi Kaal (Leg raises and sit)*

Spiritually, leg raises give us two important lessons:

1. However high the leg is raised, it has to get back to the ground, which is symbolic of the fact that whatever highs we accomplish in life, death is inevitable.
2. The raised leg represents the material growth in life, and the leg placed on the ground represents the spiritual

stability of a person. If our base leg is not grounded correctly, the more the other leg is raised, the greater the risk of falling. In the same way, however significant the material gains of life, the risk of falling is more if the spiritual base isn't proper.

Kaalugal forms a base for more advanced body-conditioning exercises like Meipayattu.

Number of leg raises practiced varies from lineage to lineage. It usually ranges from 12 to 64 in a few Kalaris.

Astha Dikh Kaalugal and *Chatur Dikh Kaalugal* (leg raises done in 8 and 4 directions keeping the raised leg in air and turning the body to all possible directions) are among the most complex leg raises a practitioner can practice.

Figure: *Sooji Kaal (Leg raises and split)*

III. Kaikuthipayattu

It is an advanced form of exercise that is part of Meithari (body form exercises). It translates to putting the hands (on the floor) exercise.

Derived from the Pillatangi sampradayam, Kaikuthipayattu is mainly practiced in the Kadathanadan region of Kerala. Pillatangi is a unique style that derives its name from a Aacharakai (hand position). The hands should be in a position of holding a baby (pilla) close to the chest. In some lineages that practice Kaikuthipayattu, technical names denote their fierce barehand applications: Ekamushti (one-fist claw) and Dasha Veral (ten-finger claw). The movements in Kaikuthipayattu are generally

Figure 12. III.a

Figure 12. III.a

Figure 12.III.a–12.III.b: *Movement in Kaikuthipayattu with different Kai Mudras*

inspired from snakes. Generally, Kaikuthipayattu is performed with various hand mudras, such as the Kutu Mushti mudra (folded hands), the Panchakai mudra (fist), and the Adikai mudra (open palm).

In Kaikuthipayattu, the practitioner moves into various postures keeping the spinal column and back in alignment, fully supported by the core region.

It increases flexibility and suppleness in the hip area and promotes correct posture.

When practiced regularly, it gives superior lower body strength and endurance. Extensive use of the four limbs of the human body (legs and hands) promotes stability in stances during actual self-defense scenarios.

The number of Kaikuthipayattu lessons or chapters depends on the individual Kalari.

IV. Meipayattu

Meipayattu is called the spine of Kalaripayattu.

It is a practice that acts as the base for the Northern style of Kalaripayattu.

It acts as an amalgamation of Vadivu Prayogam (Movements related to various combat postures), Kaalugal (leg raises), Chuvadu (footwork), and Chattankal (various complex jumps) that are endemic to Kalaripayattu.

With the practice of Meipayattu, a practitioner is said to gain the strength of an elephant, the softness of a cat, the speed of a serpent, and the grace of an antelope.

Consistent practice of Meipayattu promotes fluid movement of prana (life energy) in the body.

With leaps, low crouching stances, and continuous movement, Meipayattu prepares the students for the advanced stages of Kalaripayattu.

The complexity of jumps, leaps, and leg raises increases from lesson to lesson. The number of lessons or adavus of Meipayattu depends purely on the lineage. Number of lessons generally ranges from 12 to 18. All the movements in Meipayattu have intrinsic combat and self-defense techniques encoded within them. The Guru is an encryption key that allows the student to decode those techniques during the last stage of Kalaripayattu, Verumkai Prayogam (barehanded techniques).

Fatal attacks on Marmas (vital points) are also hidden within the movements of Meipayatt.

Meipayatt isn't just for the physical. Regular practice brings about great mind alertness, patience, control, and focus, which are the core attributes of a Kalari practitioner.

Rhythmic flow of Meipayattu accompanied with Vaaythari by the Guru brings harmony between body and mind of the practitioner.

Figure: *Advanced body-conditioning movement in Meipayattu*

V. Chummuttadi/Chuvad Adi

Chummuttadi/Chuvad Adi is a set of barehanded forms endemic to the Northern style of Kalaripayattu.

It is similar to the Chuvadu forms in the Southern style of Kalaripayattu.

It is generally done in 4 or 8 directions.

It has techniques inspired from Aswa (horse), Mayura (peacock), Sarpa (snake), and a few other animals. Vadakkan Chuvadukkal may have inspired the formulation of these techniques.

The number of lessons varies from lineage to lineage.

The Author's lineage includes 18 lessons, mainly focused on counter-attacks from mid to short range.

It also incorporates jumping and flying attacks that can be used to counter multiple-opponent scenarios.

At the advanced level, techniques are practiced with high speed and precision, making the practitioner potent against attacks in any fighting range.

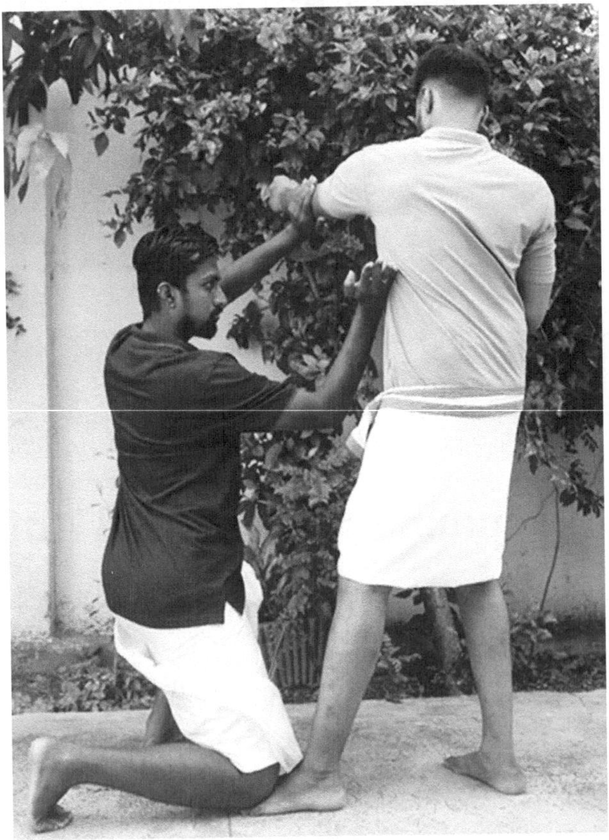

Figure: *A self-defense application present in the 6th Chummuttadi of the Author's lineage*

Figure: *An attacking Kai Mudra present in the 2nd Chummuttadi of the Author's lineage*

VI. Adithada/Kaithada

Adithada is an umbrella term used for empty-hand fighting drills used in the Southern style of Kalaripayattu.

Adi means to hit, and Thada is to block.

Kaithada is a similar system used in the Northern style of Kalaripayattu.

Both the styles incorporate choreographed fighting drills, enabling the practitioner to fight in different ranges.

The main aim of these systems is to develop reflexes and fearlessness and to condition the body to take any attack from any quarter.

The persistent practice of these techniques will help the student block attacks with relative ease, as the methods will be embossed into the muscle and subconscious memory.

In advanced stages, functional testing of these techniques in free sparring will give the practitioner a realistic view of their practical usage in life-threatening situations.

Figure: *An Adithada drill involving elbow attacks and blocks*

Figure: *A movement in the 1st Kaithada of the Author's lineage*

Adithada is also connected to and shows similarities to the barehanded practices of Kanyakumari and other Tamil martial arts.

VI. Chuvadu

Chuvadu means steps or footwork.

Kalaripayattu houses many footwork combinations with unique principles across all three geographical styles (Chapters 3 and 4).

Kalaripayattu footwork addresses all ranges (kicking range, punching range, elbow range, and grappling range).

A few commonly used Chuvadus are:

Aka chuvadu: Footstep that involves a frisk step of a small distance ready for offensive or counter-offensive movements

Neeka chuvadu: A moving step is needed to avoid an attack or counter-response

Vatta chuvadu: A parallel step, like in the elephant stance

Chatta chuvadu: A jumping step

Otta kal chuvadu: Balancing on one step

Kon chuvadu: A diagonal step

Few chuvadus are based on geometric patterns, such as Chaduram Nalu Chuvadu (square footwork) and Mukkannan Chuvadu (triangle footwork inspired from the three eyes of Lord Shiva). Many more chuvadus, such as Ankachery chuvadu (basic footwork), Balivazhy chuvadu (Monkey type footwork), Ankamvett Chuvadu (Bare hand footwork), Karinada chuvadu (Elephant footwork), Thattuvarma chuvadu (Strikes to the vital points) are also practiced in different lineages across Kerala. Few chuvadus are also connected to sacred Hindu yantras (Chapter 21.1) and characters in the Indian epics of Ramayana and Mahabharata (Hanuman Anga chuvadu, Arjunanvazhy, Bheemanvazhy and Panchali chuvadu).

Figure: *Kon chuvadu*

Figure: *Otta kal chuvadu*

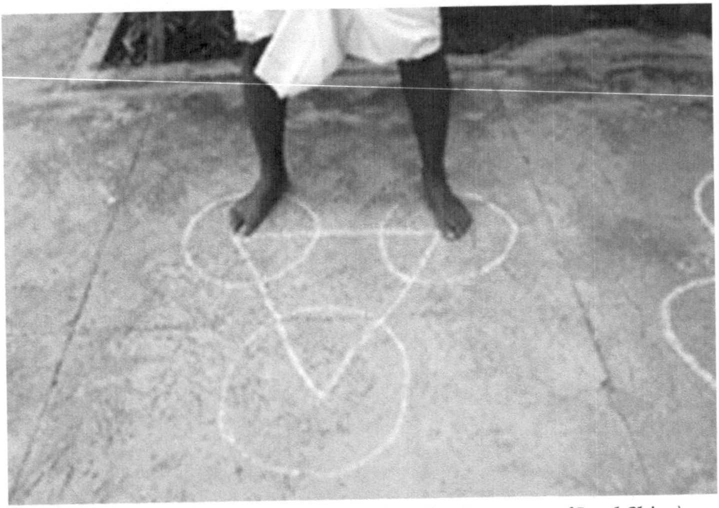

Figure: *Mukkannan chuvadu (based on the three eyes of Lord Shiva)*

VIII. Chattankal

Kalaripayattu involves many jumps to develop the practitioner's physical capability and to use them during combat.

A few Chattankal or jumps seen in Kalari are:

1. *Ottadi Pongal*: Split jump
2. *Tirinnyuchattam*: Unique side flip jump
3. *Valampiri-Idampiri*: A more advanced version of flipping one's body to the side in the air
4. *Vazhivahgi kuducchu chattam*: Evade and then a surprise jumping attack
5. *Chautti kuducchu chattam*: A jumping kick attack
6. *Kundacchattam*: Jumping attack used with a spear
7. *Odaramkandu chattam*: Jump and strike to the right side of the head.
8. *Ozhavukandu chattam:* Jump and strike to the left side of the head

Figure: *Split jump: Ottadi Pongal*

9. *Pagiritirunju chattam*: Spinning jump kick
10. *Veedu chiirukki chattam:* Jumping Inner Cresent Kick
11. *Chadikattal*: A version of it is used in Meipayattu as a rooster attack
12. *Taduttupohgal:* Block and Jump

Figure: *Tirinnyuchattam*

13

KOLTHARI: WOODEN WEAPONS

I. Kettukari Payattu

It is the first among the wooden weapons given to practitioners in Kalaripayattu, a long stick.

It is a long-range weapon usually measured from the forehead to the toe of the practitioner.

It is sometimes called Pandeeran, a short version of Pandrandu Chan (12-span stick).

Firstly, a practitioner is taught various rotations, swings, blocks, and attacks with the Vadi (stick) to gain confidence and control

Figure 13.I.a

over the weapon. This is called Vadi Veeshal or Vadiyum Chuvadum (forms with the stick).

The principles of long staff fighting vary from style to style.

In the Northern style, it is called Kettukaripayattu, Neduvadi Payattu in the Southern style, and Sharira Vadi Payattu (or Vadipayattu) in a few lineages of the Central style.

In Kettukaripayattu, a stick is held at both ends. The end with the right hand is called Amaram, and the other end with the left is called Muna.

The practitioner will be instructed never to lose contact with the stick, and both ends will be used in a sliding motion.

Two ends of the stick represent Shiva and Shakti.

Figure 13.I.b

Figure 13.I.a—13.I.b: *A blocking technique in Kettukaripayattu*

Figure: *Attacking and blocking manoeuvres in Neduvadipayattu*

A Kettukari practitioner should be able to defend and counter using both ends of the stick. Likewise, a Kalari practitioner should be able to deal with various life situations with appropriate masculine (Shiva) or feminine (Shakti) energy.

Neduvadi Payattu is correlated with the Tamil bo staff fighting style of Silambam, and it trains the student to deliver and block strikes from various grips.

Shareera Vadi Payattu is a unique style in which the attacker and the defender mostly make the same movements.

Practice with long staff will aid the practitioner to be more comfortable and proficient with the Kuntham (spear) (Chapter 14), which will be introduced to the practitioner in the later stages of learning.

II. Cheruvadi

It is a short-range weapon measuring about 40 cm, training students to deal with high-speed offensive and counter-offensive manoeuvres. It is also called Muchan (Moonu Chan), as it measures approximately three-hand spans.

Cheruvadi is generally made of tamarind wood. The end used for holding is called Amaram, and the other is called Muna. Amaram end of the stick is thicker than the Muna.

Cheruvadi involves fast-moving offensive, defensive, and counter-offensive movements, which build the student's reflexes and fearlessness in the short range.

Lessons of Cheruvadi also involve locks and disarms.

Most fatal strikes with Cheruvadi are targeted at the temple region and the crown of the head.

Low crouching stances are also adopted for short sticks engaging the core and lower body.

A specialist with this weapon can strike up to a minimum of 100 blows within a minute.

Figure: *A blocking technique with Cheruvadi*

Figure: *A stick disarm in Cheruvadi Payattu*

III. Otta

This wooden weapon is endemic to Kalaripayattu.

It is shaped like an elephant's tusk and requires much practice to attain mastery.

It is generally 18 to 20 inches long with a knob at the pointed edge, which is used to attack the vulnerable points (Marmas) in the body.

The practice of Otta gives the practitioner a deep understanding of the Marmas in the body as all attacks target the 64 Kulabhyasa Marmas (64 vital points in the human body).

It is primarily a close-range weapon, sometimes used to lock the opponent.

Figure 13. III.a

Figure 13. III.b

Figure 13. III.a–13. III.b: *Movements with the divine weapon Otta*

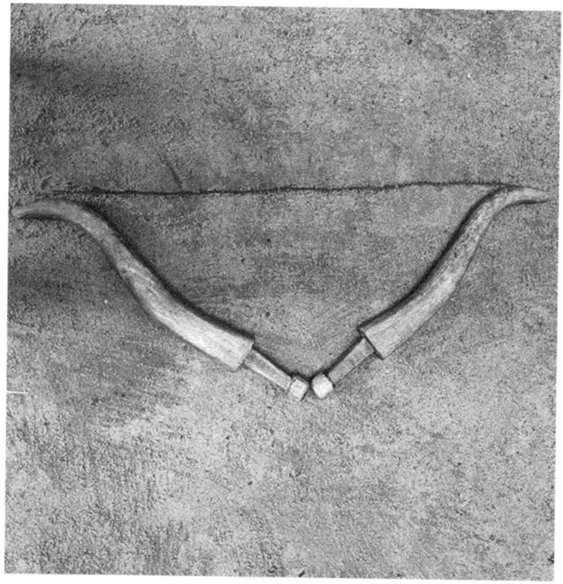

Figure: *An Otta resembles the shape of a human spinal cord. When two Ottas are joined together it takes the shape of a bow*

Movements of Otta are fluid and require much practice to attain mastery.

It is believed that Lord Krishna used an elephant's tusk to kill Kamsa, and Otta, which is generally made of tamarind wood, represents this.

Many practitioners consider the Otta a holy weapon because it symbolizes the broken tusk of Ganapathy (the Son of Lord Shiva).

One more popular story related to the origin of Ottapayattu is that Lord Shiva once roamed a forest as a hunter and saw a fight between an elephant and a lion. He observed the elephant's fighting tactics and passed on the knowledge to Sage Narada, who gave it to human beings.

Concerning Otta, it is said "Ottapayattiyal urakkathum payattam," meaning that a good practitioner of Ottapayattu can fight even when he is asleep.

These lines denote the alertness and reflexes that the practice of Otta gives the practitioner.

IV. Gadha

It is a heavy wooden weapon (generally weighing between 5 and 10 kg) and is usually wielded by well-built practitioners of Kalaripayattu. Gadha can be used for body conditioning, like a Mudgar. Attacks from a Gadha are mainly targeted at chest, ribs, temple, and head. Injuries caused by these attacking manoeuvres can be very fatal. Attacks below the waist are usually not done on moral grounds inspired by puranic stories. Indian epic characters like Lord Hanuman, Lord Balarama, Bhima, and Duryodhana were the most outstanding exponents of using the Gadha.

Figure: *Gadhapayattu (mace fight)*

V. Chottachan

In a few lineages, practitioners learn to strike or penetrate the vital spots with a small stick called Chottachan, which is designed to be easily concealed in the hand.

It is used in close-range combat scenarios.

Strikes delivered through Chottachan are mostly thrusts.

Chottachan is designed to hit the opponent with both the forehand and backhand angles.

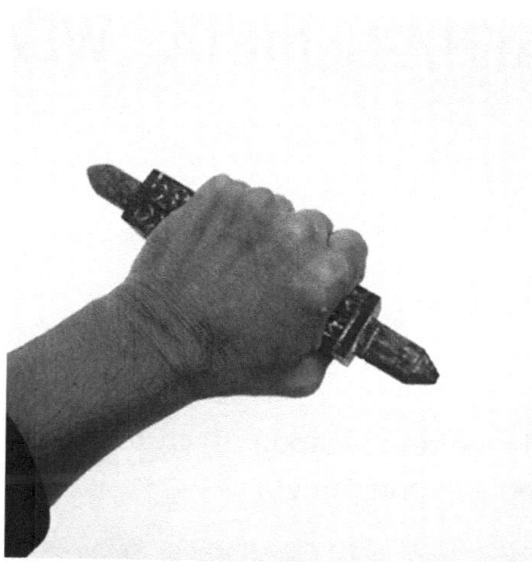

Figure: *A type of Chottachan that can deliver strikes from both the ends.*

14

ANKATHARI: METAL WEAPONS

I. Kathi

Kathi (knife) is the first weapon given to the practitioner in the metal or bladed weapon category.

Figure: *Kathipayattu practised by Ajith Gurukkal and Arun Gurukkal of Universal Kalari, Chelembra*

Knives are effective short-range weapons with great combat relevance in the contemporary world.

Through forms and pre-choreographed sequences, students are taught how to thrust, slash, and cut with single and double knives.

Later, they are taught evasive movements, disarms, and locking and unlocking techniques for knives.

Kathiyum thalayum (knives and long cloth) is a traditional Kalari practice where the attacker uses a knife and the other person uses a Thala (a piece of cloth tied to the waist or head or slung over the shoulder) to defend themselves.

This practice involves locking, choking, and throwing techniques.

Figure: *A piece of cloth used to counter a sword attack*

II. Kattaram

A Kattaram is a double-edged short-range weapon.

The weapon's construction is such that the hilt is perpendicular to the blade's longitudinal axis, enabling the practitioner to give full thrust to cut through the opponent's armor during wartime.

Figure: *Kattaram, a double edged short range weapon.*

Kattaram's lessons also involve jumping and leaping strikes accompanied by various throws.

Locking and disarming techniques are also emphasized in training.

As it is a short-range weapon, a specialist practitioner of Kattaram will be equipped with good reflexes, precision, and combat readiness.

A similar weapon is also used in Tamil martial arts and Mardhani Khel (Maratha combat style).

Figure: *A leap present in Kattarampayattu*

III. Udaval

Udaval is a bladed weapon used to counter and retaliate attacks from medium to short range.

Figure 14.III.a

Here, the blocking and attacking are done using a sword, unlike Vaalum Parichayum (Chapter 14.IV), which uses a shield along with a sword for defense or counter-attack.

Udaval practice improves the reflexes and evasion capabilities of the practitioner.

Usually, Udaval Payattu has choreographed fighting techniques, and in the advanced stages, a Guru tests the student's responsive skill with the weapon in a controlled and safe manner.

Figure 14.III.b

Figures 14.III.a–14.III.b : *Udaval Payattu*

IV. Vaalum Parichayum

Vaal means sword and Paricha is the shield.

Kalaripayattu in the contemporary world is recognized and admired through its practitioners' extraordinary sword and shield performances.

The practice of sword and shield begins with salutations to the Guru. Remembrance of Ganapati prior to the commencement of the sword session is called Ganapati anga and invoking the presiding deities of various weapons is known as Sarasvati anga. The completion of training is again concluded with special worship. The important part of sword training is the Puliyanga (Moves are inspired from Puli [tiger/leopard/panther]) and Simhatanja Valpayattu (movements inspired from lion). In most

Figure 14.IV.a

Figure 14.IV.b

Figure 14.IV.a–14.IV.b : *Puliyangam or sword and shield fighting*

of the Kalaris there is the practice of Puliyanga in which there are more jumps. Simhatanja has lower stance kind of movements.

The length of the sword is generally 40 angulam (fingerwidth) or approximately 70 cm.

Attacks with the sword involve cuts, slashes, pokes and various jumping attacking manoeuvres.

The shield is generally used for defence and sometimes for counter-offensive.

Practicing this weapon trains the student to get used to the sound of metal weapon clashing and trains them to concentrate on the attacks amidst the chaos.

A specialist in sword and shield wields both entities in a fluid, continuous and simultaneous manner.

In this fight, blocking and attacking often happens simultaneously.

The practice of sword and shield demands great agility, endurance and mind body coordination.

V. Venmazhu

Venmazhu (axe) is the weapon of the sixth avatar of Vishnu, Lord Parashurama.

Parashurama, the warrior saint, is said to be the source of the Northern style of Kalaripayattu.

But, nowadays, fighting with axe is practiced more in the Southern and Central styles of Kalaripayattu.

Axe is a weapon that can chop through a protective armor during warfare.

An axe can break through bones and rip through muscles.

Few lineages of Southern style of Kalaripayattu have choreographed forms concerning the axe from which the student learns to evade attacks from an axe and disarms associated with it.

Figure: *Parashurama, the sixth avatar of Mahavishnu with his weapon Axe.*

VI. Kuntham

A spear is called Kuntham in Malayalam and Vel Kambu in Tamil.

It is believed that Kuntham or Vel Kambu is a representation of the Vel in the hands of Lord Karthikeya.

Kuntham Payattu (Kundapayattu), or spear fight, is part of the advanced stages of Ankathari.

A practitioner with a spear generally trains to do pokes, slashes to the muscles, or strikes to the bones and crown of the head. In the short range, the holding end of the spear can also be used for tricky or deceiving strikes.

Students are taught to handle the spear against an opponent with a sword and shield or double swords. The sword and shield are occasionally replaced with short sticks and the spear with a long cane. Such a practice is called Kundakettukaari or Kundam kuruvadi.

Figure 14.VI.a

Figure 14.VI.b

Figures 14.VI.a – 14.VI.b : *Demonstration of attacking techniques with the spear and countering them using sword and shield*

Kuntham, a long-range weapon, is effective against fending off mob attacks or multiple attackers.

A fight with sword (Vaal) and spear (Kuntham) is known as Mara Pidicha Kuntham.

VII. Urumi

Urumi is a flexible whip-like double-edged blade mainly used to counter multiple attackers.

It is one of the last weapons taught in Kalaripayattu, as it requires extreme mastery of the weapon and oneself.

If not used carefully, it can injure the person swinging it.

Figure: *Urumi Veeshal done with both hands*

In the olden days, it was worn around the waist like a belt and taken out when there were mob attacks.

To master the swings, the practitioners learn to wield a single Urumi first and then advances to double Urumi, one in each hand (Urumi Veeshal).

Then they advance to Urumipayattu (fighting with Urumi), where they defend themselves using a shield and attacks using the Urumi against a single or multiple opponents.

Figure: *Prakash Gurukkal of Prasarana Kalari, Bengaluru, demonstrating a posture within the lessons of Urumipayattu*

15

VERUMKAI PRAYOGAM: UNARMED COMBAT

Although this is considered the final stage in Kalaripayattu, it is closely related to the previous stages. The intricate combat details of the body-conditioning forms practiced by the practitioner are explained by the Guru. Techniques of locking and unlocking (Poottu-Pirivu) an opponent and disarming a weapon using bare hands are taught. Detailed explanations of footwork patterns and the importance of precision are provided. The art of targeting specific Marmas (vulnerable points) (Chapter 16) using appropriate hand gestures (Kai Mudras) (Chapter 17) are revealed to the students. Various throws, evasions, and asymmetrical strikes that can effectively incapacitate an opponent are imparted to disciplined students under the strict supervision of the master. Students take an oath on their father, mother, teacher, Kalari, and the Almighty God that they won't use this knowledge for evil intentions. In some lineages of Kalaripayattu where weapon training is minimal, emphasis will be given to the art of barehanded fighting from the beginning of the training. Still, the secrets of the forms will only be revealed after gaining the master's trust. Each style, lineage, and master will have a confidential set of techniques, which the teacher will pass down to a select few trustworthy disciples.

Figure 15.1

I. Inner nuances of Verumkai Prayogam

As per a few lineages of the Northern Style of Kalaripayattu, Verumkai Prayogam can be divided into four parts :

1. *Kaiyum Kaiyum* (Hand to Hand Combat)
2. *Kambum Kaiyum* (Barehand techniques against an opponent with a stick or an impact weapon)
3. *Kathiyum Talayum* (Techniques using a rope or cloth against an opponent with a knife or any other weapon)
4. *Kathiyum Kaiyum* (Barehand techniques against an opponent who uses a knife or a bladed weapon)

1) Kaiyum Kaiyum

It is also known as Muşti Yuddham or Kaiyum Meiyum, where the practitioner and his opponent/s are without weapons, and the practitioner defends only by using body limbs.

It has 12 sub-divisions:

i) Tadavugal (Blocks)

ii) Upatadavugal (Sub-Blocks)

iii) Mattangal (Evasions)

iv) Kayattangal (Moving into attack)

v) Vettugal (Open-Handed Chopping techniques)

vi) Idigal (Punching techniques)

vii) Chavuttugal (Kicking techniques)

viii) Tattugal (Tapping techniques leading to pushing, pulling, or throws)

ix) Pidigalum Poottugalum (Holds and Locking techniques)

x) Yerugal (Moving in and Throwing techniques)

xi) Tadavillakkaigal (Counter-attacking Techniques)

xii) Marmakkaigal (Attacking the Marma points)

i. Tadavugal

These are blocks that are used when an opponent attacks. There are eight such blocks: Nilayil Tada, Ayamtalli Tada, Agankai Tada, Purankai Tada, Kaipinacchu Tada, Agankal Tada, Purankal Tada and Matta Tada.

ii. Upatadavugal

These are sub-blocks or deflections of attacks.

There are eight such blocks: Adangal Tada, Marma Tada, Akamvetti Tada, Irrukkai Tada, Varittada, Amarttitada Valathupukkutada, and Idattupukkutada.

iii. Mattangal

These techniques are used when one is unable to judge or defend the opponent's attack. An effective counter-attack is done with turns and twists that confuse the opponent.

There are six main sub-divisions here: Tattimattam, Chuvadumattam, Anjumattam, Nirangimattam, Chadimattam, Urundamattam.

iv. Kayattangal

The practitioner moves to the right or left side or straight into the opponent with an appropriate attack.

There are three different types of applications:

1. Anjukayattam
2. Kettikayattam
3. Teritthukayattam.

v. Vettugal

These are open-handed chopping techniques.

The hand is directed either upward or downward. In vettugal both hands are used. The name of the vettugal is based on the consequences caused by the damage of the marma points, such as Rakktacheetti (gushing of blood), and Kaitalarpam (paralyzing hand).

vi. Idigal

These are punch-like techniques delivered using the practitioner's fist, elbow, knee, or head.

vii. Chavuttugal

This refers to using feet to hit or push the opponent. The ridge of the foot is used excessively in Chavuttu. The sole and the ball of the foot (the area above the sole) are also used to hit and push the opponent. The attack is aimed at the navel, stomach, rib, testicle, knees, thighs, face, or the chest.

Some well-known techniques are Valampiri and Idampiri, Nerkana, Pinchavuttu, Irittichavuttu, etc.

Figure 15.2

viii. Tattugal

Tattu means tapping. These techniques include pulling, pushing, and throwing. Here, the opponent's speed and strength are used against himself. The defender achieves this by using the leg to imbalance and push the opponent to the floor. This is one of the most dangerous forms of Verumkai if skillfully applied. The application of this technique is mostly below the knees.

Some techniques are Ganapatikai, Hanumankai, Bhimankai, Bālikai, etc.

ix. Pidigalum-Poottugalum:

These are holding, restraining and locking techniques. Using one hand is pidi and holding the opponent with both hands is called poottu. The locks produce pain and make the opponent immobile.

There are many kinds, and some that can be easily applied are Nakshatram Noki Poothu, Katrikapoottu, Madhallam Kaatti Poothu, Kupra, Eratta Kupra, etc.

If more power is applied to such locks, bone breaking or joint dislocations are possible.

Figure 15.3

x. Yerugal

These are techniques of approaching the opponent and 'throwing.' The approach is either towards the right or left side of the opponent, grasping his shoulder, back, or hip and throwing.

There are 12 such divisions here: Minnikkai, Valicchuyeru, Chuttiveeshiyeru, Hastachakra, Andamalakkam, Valampagiritirucchеru, Idampagiritiruccheru, Valaveeshiyeru, Peruntadaiyeru, Kundamchatti, Kavaniyeru and Agamvalicchuyeru.

xi. Tadavillakaigal

Here, the opponent's attack is rendered useless by an immediate counter-attack, which prevents the opponent from applying a defense mechanism.

xii. Marmakkaigal

As the name indicates, these techniques are used to attack the Marma points. The teaching combines not only the way of damaging the Marma points but also how to cure the affected one. The technique of Marmakkaigal is applied using various parts of the hand, leg, elbow, shoulder, head, and knee. Some of the techniques of application with hand are Vettikkai, Anikkai, Kundakkai, Aravakkai, Simhakkai, Mustikkai, Chuttikkai, Pārakkai, Vajrakkai, etc. These are kept as secrets and are taught only to the most eligible students.

Kottukol

The use of a small stick for striking the Marma points is known as Kottu Vidyā. The technique of using it is taught as part of Marmakkaigal. This stick is also known as Kottukol or Marmavadi. It is small in size and can be held within the palm.

2) Kambum Kaiyum

These are a compilation of barehand defensive and counter-offensive techniques against opponents who advance with a stick or any such impact weapon.

Figure 15.4

Figures 15.a—15d: *A sneak peek into various throwing, locking, offensive and counter-offensive techniques under the umbrella of Verumkai Prayogam*

3) Kathiyum Talayum

A rope or a piece of cloth is used for defense when an opponent attacks with a knife or any such weapon. The rope or cloth (tala) is used to defend, dodge, and move away or lock the opponent.

4) Kathiyum Kaiyum

These are barehand techniques used against an opponent who wields a knife. The techniques such as tadavu, olavu, pidigal are used. A blunt knife is used in initial practice sessions. There are 8 tadavus: Odiramtada, Olavutada, Varitada, Maruvaritada, Ezhikkukeetatada, Araikkikeezhatada, Nerodirama and Odakkuneetti.

Dodging or methods of avoiding strikes from the knife are Pinmättam, Teruttumatti Ozhijnu, Nilayayil-amarndu-ozhijnu and Tattiozhijnu.

Techniques of grabbing the knife from the opponent are Kattikai, Kavarankayitti, Kazhuttu-ketti, Kallanketti, Adivari, Pinvari, Pudappalaki, Kaipidicchu-ganapati-tattu and Anairutti.

II. Mantra Sadhana

Mantra Sadhana is given great importance in some lineages of Kalaripayattu as it helps elevate the practitioner spiritually. Mantras directly impact the physical and subtle bodies, forming a spiritual shield around the practitioner. This shield protects the practitioner from evil eyes, occult practices, and also enhances intuitive capabilities.

In addition to Vadivu mantram (mantras chanted with various postures), masters also practiced five different mantras to be used in fighting:

1. Sivakkaruttu mantram (mild encounters)
2. Bhadrakali mulamantram (angry or heated encounters)
3. Hanuman mulamantram (jumping to attack or defend)
4. Virabhadra mulamantram (when it is necessary to kill an opponent)

5. Pasupadam (Siva's) mantram (to charm a weapon)

Some lineages also practice general, all-purpose mantram to access higher powers rather than powers specific to a technique or weapon. Mantras associated with Bhagavati, Hanuman, Ganapathy, and past Gurus are commonly practiced.

The Guru Mantra holds profound significance in the traditional training process. Before imparting knowledge of any new weapon to a student, the Guru silently chants this sacred mantra. This practice is believed to invoke divine blessings, ensuring the safety of both teacher and student while minimizing the risk of injuries during practice.

The use of various yogic bandhas like mulabandam, uddiyanabandam, and jalandrabandam with the chanting of the sacred syllable "OM" or "AUM" while holding the various mudras can also be observed in a few lineages.

16

KALARI CHIKITSA

Kalaripayattu is a unique and ancient martial art system that focuses not only on combat, but also on understanding the profound workings of the human body and its relationship with nature. By doing so, practitioners can become Kalaripayattu masters who can heal ailments that prevent the human body from realizing its true potential and living a healthy life. This understanding also allows a Kalaripayattu master to heal injuries during combat training. The Northern styles of Kalaripayattu base their healing techniques on the science of Ayurveda, while the Southern style relies on the Siddha Medicine system. Kalari treatment, known as Kalari Chikitsa, emphasizes harmonizing the flow of Prana (life force) to heal ailments. Knowledge of the flow of Prana in Nadis and its corresponding physical energy centers (Marmas) will enable a Kalari master to cure diseases and, in extreme situations, use it to harm an opponent fatally. Kalari Chikitsa aims to repair and rejuvenate the body by balancing the Tridosha (Vata, Pitta, and Kapha) through proper diet, medicines, and massages. It involves several specific massage therapies, such as Uzhichil, Kizhithirumu, and Chavutti Thirummal, which can benefit the body in various ways.

Uzhichil is a massage therapy that aids in revitalizing the neuro-muscular system of the body. It promotes rejuvenation of the body by stimulating blood circulation, and the massages are

Figure: *Kalari Uzhichil*

performed with medicinal oils. Most of the times, these oils are prepared by the masters, using ancient wisdom passed down through generations.

Kizhithirumu therapy is a massage in which specially prepared herbs and leaves are put into a small cloth sack known as a Kizhi.

The cloth bags are dipped into medicated oil (Thailam) and then applied to the patient's body. The combination of medicated oils and herbs used on the patient is also determined according to body type and the ailment. The Kizhi is applied with appropriate pressure to the parts of the body where there is pain or swelling.

Chavutti Thirummal is a full-body massage where the massager uses their feet for the central part of the treatment. The therapist supports themselves with a rope suspended from the ceiling, allowing continuous massage strokes with the leg. The neck, face, and head are massaged using only the hands. There is also a saying that viruses fear entering a body massaged by a foot.

These massages are done for 7, 14, or 21 days to balance the Tridosha by eliminating toxins.

Kalari Chikitsa is also used to treat orthopaedic ailments like fractures, dislocations, sprains, joint pains, arthritis, and many other bodily issues, making it an excellent holistic system for healing physical and mental ailments.

Kalaripayattu demands that practitioners understand the human body and its relationship with nature. This enables them to stay connected to the nature and be one with it over time.

Knowledge of Tridosha, Panchindriya, Pancha Mahabuta, Nadis, and Vayus is necessary for a Kalari practitioner to transcend into the next level of awareness.

I. Nadis

Prana shakti, or pranic energy, flows through the subtle body in a network of pranic currents called Nadis.

Nadi, in Sanskrit, means channel. Within the human body, a network of 72,000 Nadis distributes Prana effectively throughout the body, of which 14 are of paramount importance.

The *Darshana Upanishad* mentions: "The Nadi located in the middle of the knot of the navel is Sushumna. Seventy-two thousand Nadis stand around it. Among them, fourteen Nadis are important."

Ancient Yoga sources agree that all the Nadis have their starting point in the Kanda (also referred to as Kandasthana), that is, in the navel area or lower abdominal area. Classical texts also mention that the Nadis originate in the heart region.

The fourteen important Nadis and their commonly accepted endpoints are:

	Nadi	Ending point
1.	Sushumna	Crown of the head (also called Brahmarandhra)
2.	Ida	Left nostril
3.	Pingala	Right nostril
4.	Gandhari	Left eye
5.	Hastijihva	Right eye
6.	Yashaswini	Left ear
7.	Pusha ends	Right ear
8.	Alambusha	Mouth and alternatively ends in the anus
9.	Kuhu	Genitals
10.	Shankhini	Anus
11.	Payaswini	Right ear
12.	Saraswati	Mouth (tip of the tongue)
13.	Varuna	Extends throughout the entire body, connected with the feet (toes), hands (fingers), and the skin
14.	Vishvodhara	Resides within the Kanda (navel area).

Out of the 14, three Nadis, Ida, Pingala, and Sushumna are important.

- Ida is the subtle body's passive, feminine, yin energy channel. It lies to the left of Sushumna Nadi and is also known as Chandra Nadi.
- Pingala is the subtle body's masculine, active yang energy channel. It lies to the right of Sushumna Nadi. It is also called Surya Nadi.
- Sushumna is the neutral energy channel that passes through the spine in the subtle body. The sacred text of *Lalitha Sahasranama* (devoted to Goddess Shakthi) speaks about the presence of Vajra Nadi and Chitra Nadi within Sushumna.

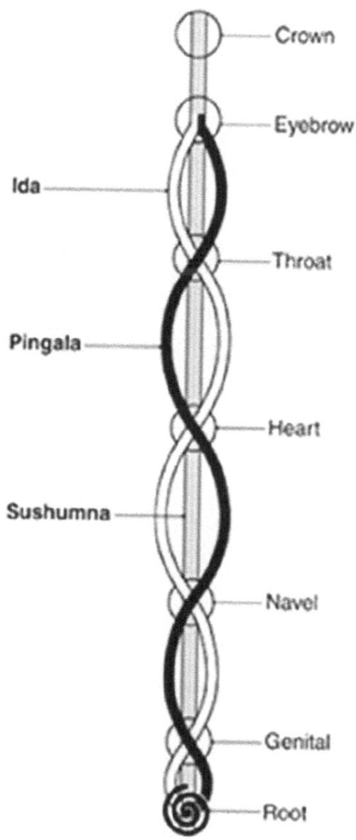

Figure: *Three important Nadis: Ida , Pingala, and Sushumna*

Balancing the masculine and feminine energies, or Pingala and Ida, facilitates the awakening and rising of Kundalini shakti through Sushumna and, thus, the awakening of higher consciousness.

II. Pancha Mahabhuta and Tridosha

Earth (Prithvi), Water (Jala), Fire (Agni), Ether (Akasha), and Air (Vayu) constitute the cosmos and the human body.

The unique interplay of these elements within the human body determines one's Prakriti.

This unique constitution determines an individual's physical, mental, and emotional characteristics and disease susceptibility through three fundamental energies called Tridosha: Vata, Pitta, and Kapha.

Vata: Vata comprises the air and ether elements. It regulates thoughts, emotions, and bodily functions. Excess of Vata can lead to anxiety, dryness, and nervous disorders.

Pitta: Pitta is made of the fire and water elements. It regulates metabolism, digestion, and the transformation of food into energy. However, excess Pitta can lead to irritability, inflammation, and digestive problems.

Kapha: Kapha is composed of water and earth elements. It regulates stability, strength, and lubrication in the body. Excess of Kapha can lead to lethargy, weight gain, and congestion.

With proper diet, lifestyle, and regular practice of Kalaripayattu, one can balance the Tridosha and be free from ailments.

III. Chakras

Chakras are energy centers within the subtle body. Some believe there are 114 Chakras, but seven are considered prime importance. They are:

1. Muladhara Chakra - Root Chakra
2. Swadishtana Chakra - Sacral Chakra
3. Manipura Chakra - Solar Plexus Chakra
4. Anahata Chakra - Heart Chakra
5. Vishuddhi Chakra - Throat Chakra
6. Ajna Chakra - Third Eye Chakra
7. Sahasrara Chakra - Crown Chakra

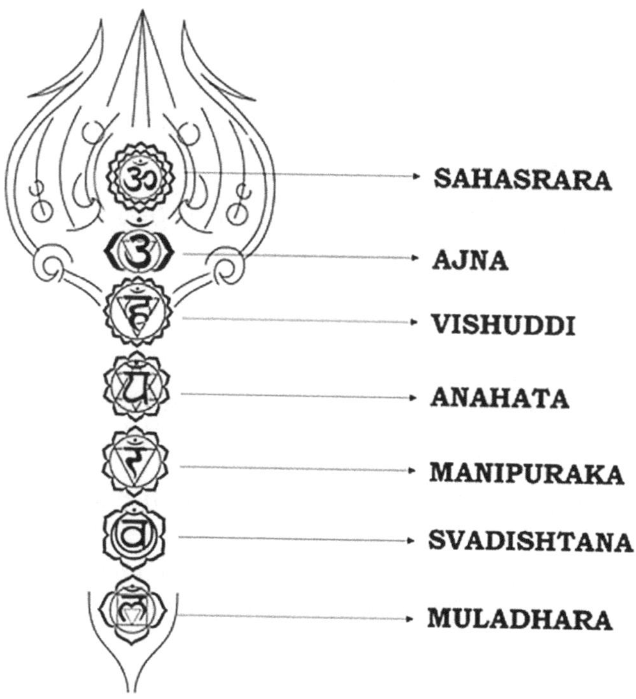

Figure: *Seven important chakras*

Each Chakra is connected to the Tridosha, Pancha Vayu, Pancha Mahabhuta, and overall to Marmas (vital points).

IV. Marmas

Marmas are vital points in the body where the Prana Shakti, or energy (life force), is concentrated or encircled along the complex system of subtle channels called Nadis.

They can be used either to heal or to fatally hurt a person.

The word Marma or Marmam means secret or essence in Sanskrit.

It is also called Varmam in the Tamil lineage of martial arts.

In the Southern style of Kalaripayattu, the system of 108 main Marmas is followed. This system is based on the principles of Siddha Medicine.

The 108 Marmas are divided into two segments based on the concentration of pranic energy at the point.

Centers where high pranic energy is concentrated are called Padu Varmam.

Energy centers with less concentration of pranic energy than Padu Varmam are called Thodu Varmam.

Padu Varmam is 12 in number and Thodu Varmam is 96 in number.

These Varmam points are connected and dependent on

1. Charam (understanding the flow of breath)
2. Panchapakshi Shastra (study of connection of the five elements to five different birds [Peacock, Vulture, Cock, Crow, and Owl] and its connection to the human body. It is also used as a method of astrology)
3. Nadis (subtle channels present in the human body carrying the pranic energy)

4. Amritham and Visham (understanding the flow of nectar and toxins in the body corresponding to the waxing and waning of the moon).

The study of Marmas on the principles of Siddha Medicine is a complex and exhaustive science.

The Northern style of Kalaripayattu mainly follows the system of 64 Kulabhyasa Marmas.

(a) 64 Kulabhyasa Marmas

Body parts	Number of Marmas
Hand	12 (6 + 6)
Legs	10 (5 + 5)
Stomach	3
Chest	12
Back	7
Throat	7
Head	13

HAND

- Viralooni: Present in the hand at the confluence of the thumb and index finger
- Naadipathi: At the middle of the forearm
- Kai Kuzhappan: Near the elbow
- Kaithooki: Located in the biceps
- Kaitharippan: Located at the shoulder joint
- Phanam: Located at the armpit

LEGS

- Nadathalappan: Located near the foot
- Vaayupodi: Located at the back of the knee
- Kaal Thookhi: Located at the back of the thighs
- Aanavaari: Located above the knee on the side tracks of the thighs
- Ottukuvaliyan: Located at the upper part of the thigh

STOMACH

- Malapindam: One middle finger above the navel
- Jalapindam: One index finger below the navel
- Urulmani: One thumb distance below Jalapindam

CHEST

- Trishangu Pushpam: In between the two chest nipples
- Thilakkuzhi: Located in the chest cavity, one index finger below Trishangu Pushpam
- Rakthamthuppi: They are 4 in number. One finger above and below the chest nipples
- Swasamadappan: It is located in the line of the nipples at the side of the chest
- Rohitham: Below the collarbone
- Nooluvalippan: Located two fingers below Rohitham

BACK

- Tarippan: It's on the rib cage, four and a half fingers below Swasamadappan.
- Kondakolli: Located three fingers below Tarippan

- Atta Churutti: Present near the ribs; located three fingers below kondakolli
- Urakkam Thooki: Located at the confluence of neck and shoulder

NECK

- Chumayan: In the valve below the throat
- Nakshatram Nokki: Above the Adam's apple
- Kazhuthuthooki: Four fingers above Urakkam Thooki
- Muradanakki: Located in the valve behind the earlobes
- Kazhthukochi: Located in the valve behind the collarbone

HEAD

- Vayuchinni: Located at the centre of the head
- Trikoodakyam: Located between the eyebrows
- Naaku Tharippan: Located below the mouth
- Kannudhi: Located in the cavity next to the eyes
- Sirashraya: Located a thumb far diagonally above Kannundi
- Mookadappan: Located in the cavity next to the nose lobes
- Vaythurappan: Located on the cheeks
- Chirikodan: It is located diagonally below the ears at the jaw

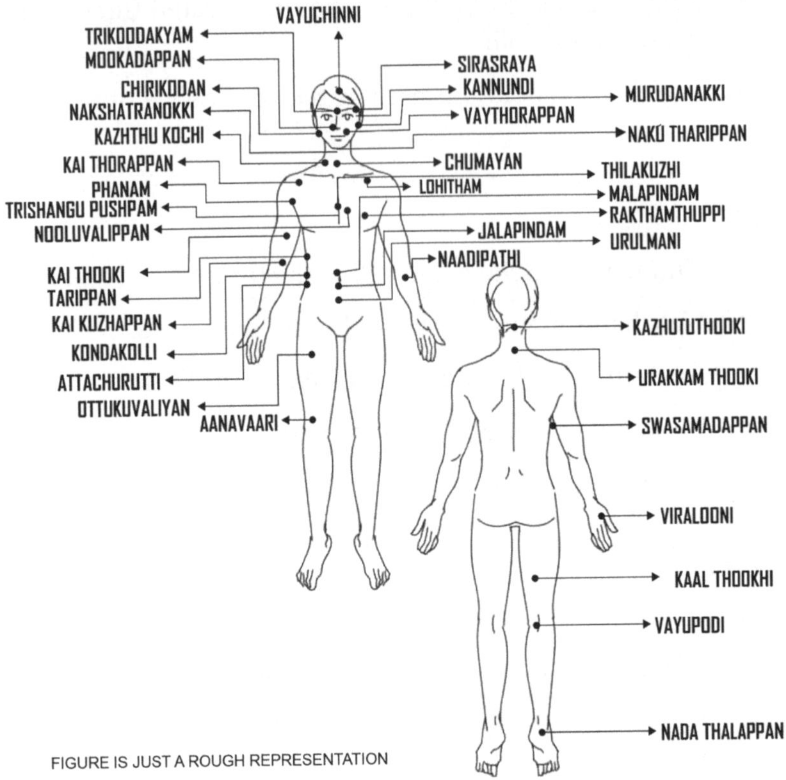

Figure: *Rough representation of 64 Kulabhyasa marmas*

In Ayurveda, the body contains 107 recognized marma points, which are categorized according to different aspects and were primarily documented by Acharya Sushruta and Acharya Vagbhatta. The categorizations include:

1. Area Classification (Shadang Bhedena)
2. Structural Classification (Rachana Bhedena)
3. Outcome Classification (Parinaama Bhedena)
4. Quantity Classification (Sankhya Bhedena)
5. Numerical Classification (Parimaana Bhedana)

According to the structural classification (Rachana Bhedena), the 107 marma points in the body are divided into five anatomical classes or marma types:

- Mamsa marma: Muscular spots
- Sira marma: Venous spots
- Snayu marma: Ligamental spots
- Asthi marma: Bony spots
- Sandhi marma: Spots in joints

The Astanga Hridaya added a sixth type, dhamani marma, representing arterial spots.

Name of Marma	As per Sushruta	As per Vagbhatta
Mamsa Marma	11	10
Sira Marma	41	37
Snayu Marma	27	23
Asthi Marma	08	08
Sandhi Marma	20	20
Dhamani Marma	-	09
Total	**107**	**107**

Marmas can also be categorized as Thodu Marmam (attacked by touching), Choondu Marmam (attacked by pointing the index finger at the opponent's marmas), and Noku Marmam (attacking by looking).

Using Choondu Marma and Noku Marma to disable an opponent requires psychic powers derived from mantra and tantra sadhana.

The particular mantras and the way of invoking them to harness subtle energies are kept secret and are passed down from the Guru to the most level-headed and disciplined disciples.

It is said

Marmam Parpadarkhu
Manamadile Adakkam Venum
Poornamayi Shiva Shakti Dhyanam Venum
Ulagathandril pala uyirum ondradagi
Thappamal Dhayanam adhu
Palinthinythu

Practitioners of marma science should have complete control over their mind and body.

They should understand and meditate on Shiva (masculine energy) and Shakti (feminine energy).

To realize the ultimate reality, they should see the presence of Paramatma (Universal Consciousness) in every Jeevaatma (Individual Consciousness).

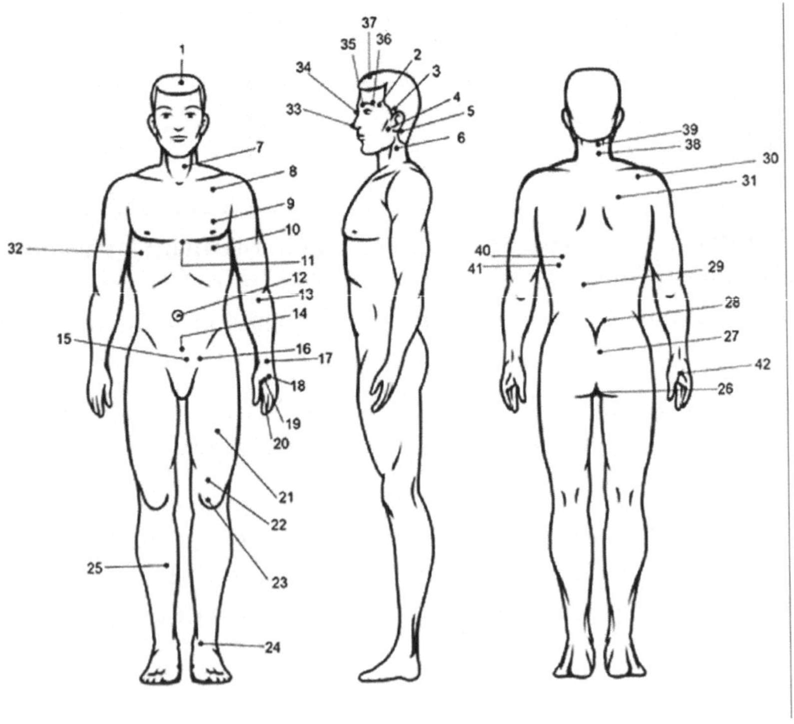

Figure 16. a: *The Locations of marmason the body as per a kalaripayatu text, the MARMMANIDANAM*

Table: *Names of the Marmas in the figure*

1. Adipati	2. Samkhannal	3. Ulksepannal
4. Sramgatannal	5. Vidyara	6. Manya
7. Nila	8. Kaksyadhrka	9. Stanarohitam
10. Hrdayam	11. Stanamulam	12. Nabhi
13. Korpparam	14. Vasti	15. Pitivam
16. Lohitaksham	17. Manibanham	18. Kurccasirassu
19. Kurccam	20. Ksipram	21. Urvvi
22. Ani	23. Janu	24. Gulpam
25. Indravasti	26. Gudamarmmam	27. Nitambannai
28. Katikataryanannai	29. Parswasndhikal	30. Amsannal
31. Amsaphalnnal	32. Avastambha	33. Phalannai
34. Sthapani	35. Apamgannal	36. Avarttanal
37. Simanannal	38. Matrakal	39. Krkatika
40. Brhati	41. Apalapannal	42. Talahrtta

The science of Marma Shastra is not just about hitting and healing; it also enables the practitioner to transcend the physical body and become one with the cosmos.

Practical usage of Marma strikes requires a lot of practice.

When fighting a skilled, moving opponent, executing a vital point strike in that adrenaline rush requires much functional sparring.

17

KAI MUDRAS

Kalaripayattu has various Kai mudras (hand gestures) to attack the marmas depending on their location and depth.

A few commonly used Kai mudras across all styles are: Yaanaimukham mudra (Elephant face), Aswamukham mudra (Horse face), Shakti mudra (Open hand), Varaha mudra (Elbow), Trishula mudra (Lord Shiva's Trident), Chakra mudra (Lord Vishnu's Sudarshana Chakra), Pancha mudra (Tiger claw), Tembukai mudra (Scooping hands), Kutumushti mudra (Folded hands), Panchakai mudra (Fist), Adikai mudra (Open palm), Vettukai mudra (Cutting hand), Tettakai mudra (Elbow).

Using a particular Mudra for different Marmas might not be uniform across all Kalaris.

To hurt a particular marma with precision, the practitioner should know the appropriate Kai Mudra, Marma Disha (direction of force), and the pressure required to hit (Azhutha Matra and Pathi Matra).

Figure: *Chakra Mudra, inspired from Lord Vishnu controlling his Sudarshana Chakra in his index finger.*

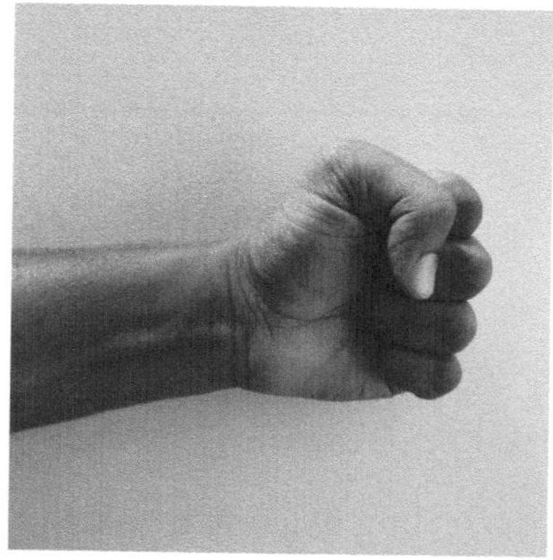

Figure: *Panchakai mudra*

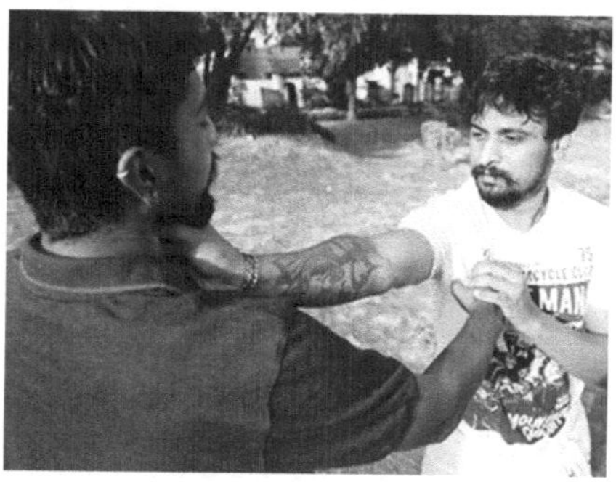

Figure: *Trishula mudra*

Figure: *Varaha mudra*

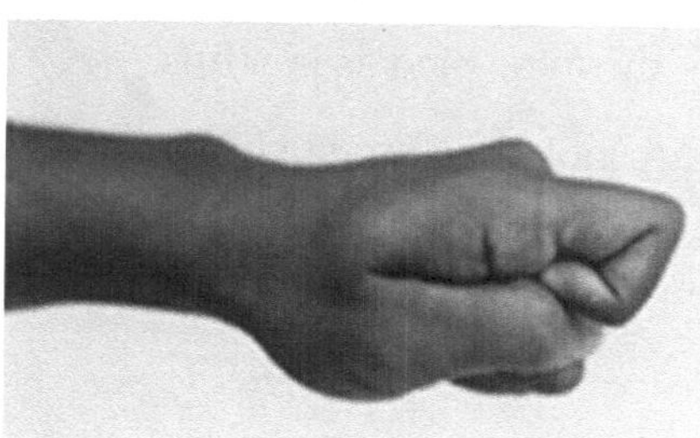

Figure: *Aswamukha mudra*

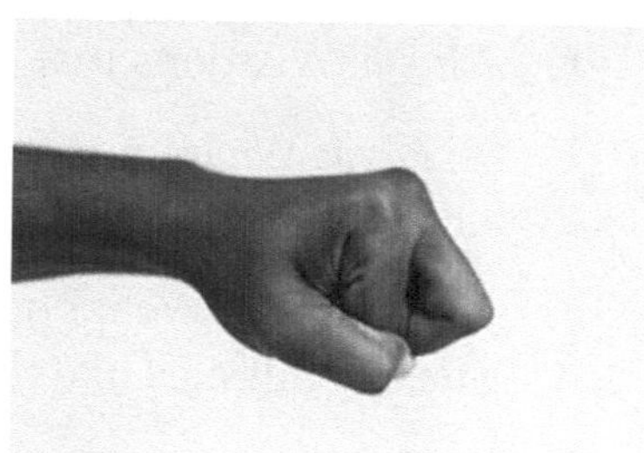

Figure: *Yaanai mukha mudra*

18

DHANURVEDIC CONNECT

According to a few masters, Kalaripayattu has strong connection to the *Dhanurveda,* a scientific treatise on the art of warfare in India.

Both Parashurama and Agasthya, the founders of the Northern and Southern style of Kalaripayattu, respectively, have strong connection to the ancient Vedic culture.

Vishnu Purana mentions *Dhanurveda* to be one of the 18 branches of knowledge.

Agni Purana also mentions *Dhanurveda* and its inner branches.

Dhanurveda is an Upaveda (subversion) of *Yajur Veda,* which allows practitioners to become skilled in the science of combat and its inner nuances. According to *Dhanurveda,* using bows and arrows is considered the superior mode to other forms of combat. Unarmed fighting is considered to be the least desirable.

According to *Dhanurveda,* weapons are categorized into four types based on their nature:

1. *Mukta*: Weapons that are thrown, such as javelins.
2. *Amukta*: Weapons that are not thrown, such as swords and thunderbolts.
3. *Muktamukta*: Weapons that can be thrown or not thrown, such as missiles like the *Nāgāstra* and *Garuḍāstra.*

4. *Yantramukta*: Weapons that are thrown by spells or machines, such as catapult balls and arrows shot from a bow.

Figure: *Dhanurvidya*

Dhanurveda also classifies weapons based on how they are released:

1. *Panimukta*: Weapons thrown directly by hand, such as stones and spears.
2. *Mantramukta*: Weapons thrown with the power of mantras, such as the *Brahmastra* and *Pāśupatāstra*.

Many popular sports described in the Vedas and epics have their origins in military training, such as Boxing (*Mushti-Yuddha*), Wrestling (*Mal, Dvandhva Yudh*), Chariot-racing (*Ratha Chalan*), Horse-riding (*Ashva-Rohan*), and Archery (*Dhanurvidya*).

Dhanurveda describes the rules, practices, and uses of archery, bow-and-arrow making, and military training. The text also elaborates on the training of warriors, charioteers, horseriders, elephant warriors, and infantry.

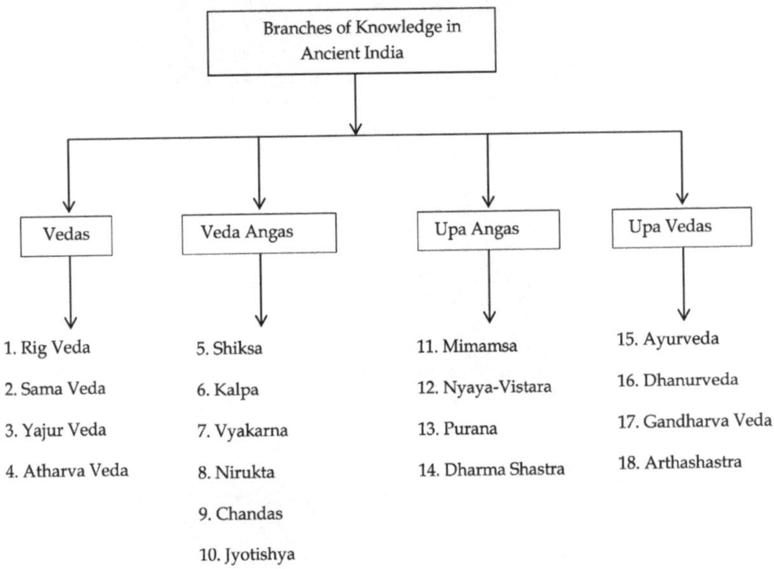

Figure: *Eighteen branches of knowledge in ancient India.*

19

GURU-SHISHYA RELATIONSHIP

The very base of Kalaripayattu is the relationship between the Guru and the disciple.

The word "Guru" is derived from two words: Gu and Ru. "Gu" means darkness or ignorance, and "Ru" means dispeller. Here, a Guru is someone who dispels darkness and guides the disciples through the principles of Kshatra Dharma. The knowledge transfer is very subjective to the behaviour of the student.

Figure 19.a

Figure 19.b

Figures 19.a.—19.b : *A teacher guides the disciple to gain mastery over the mind and body*

The Guru serves as a catalyst in a student's life, facilitating their transformation from a layman to a courageous warrior, both physically and mentally.

Among many mentions in Hindu culture about the significance of and importance given to a Guru, I provide two chants here.

Guru Brahma,

Guru Vishnu,

Guru Devo Maheshwarah!

Guru Saakshaat Parabrahma,

Tasmai Shri Guruve Namah!

Meaning

The Guru is Brahma (The God of Creation)

The Guru is Vishnu (The God of Sustenance)

The Guru is Shiva (The God of Annihilation)

My Salutation to such a Guru, who is like the Supreme God.

Tvameva Mata Cha Pita Tvameva |

Tvameva Bandhush-Cha Sakha Tvameva |

Tvameva Vidyaa Dravinnam Tvameva |

Tvameva Sarvam Mama Deva | |

Meaning

You [Guru] are mother and father to me

You are only my relative and my friend

You are my wisdom and my wealth

You are everything for me, Oh God of Gods

20

KACHAKETTAL

After reaching a certain level of practice (in the Author's lineage: 5th Adavu or 5th level of body-conditioning exercises), a Kalari practitioner is presented with a traditional dress called a Kacha by his/her Guru on an auspicious day. Kacha is a piece of cloth generally one span width and 24 forearm measures in length. It is worn above the loincloth tightly to protect the navel region, lower back (the tailbone), and genital area.

Figure: *Kachakettal*

As the navel region is considered to be the source of Prana Shakti, Kacha acts as a protection to it.

The Kacha is often complexly wound around the waist, hip, and genital region.

The process of wearing or tying this traditional dress of Kacha is called Kachakettal.

21

KALAM CHAVITT

Kalam Chavitt is a unique and lethal system based on geometric footwork patterns and body alignment for combat.

It is an umbrella term that generally denotes combat practices in geometric patterns that arise in South India. In Kerala, it was mainly practiced by the local natives, who were also influenced by regional tribal combat knowledge. Tactics used to trap animals were metamorphosed to take down human attackers.

Here, the practitioner moves according to 'Kalams' drawn on the floor or creates a pattern with his/her footwork.

If the practitioner places his/her foot in two places, it is Thanne Kalam (Two Kalam).

If three spots are stepped upon, then it is Moonu Kalam (Three Kalam).

Kalam Chavitt is generally a journey from one Kalam to sixty-four Kalam, which involves various geometric patterns.

The system is mainly built on Chaduram Nalu (square footwork), Mookalam (forward and reverse triangle footwork), Vatta Chuvadu (circular footwork), and Thanne Kalam (Two Kalam).

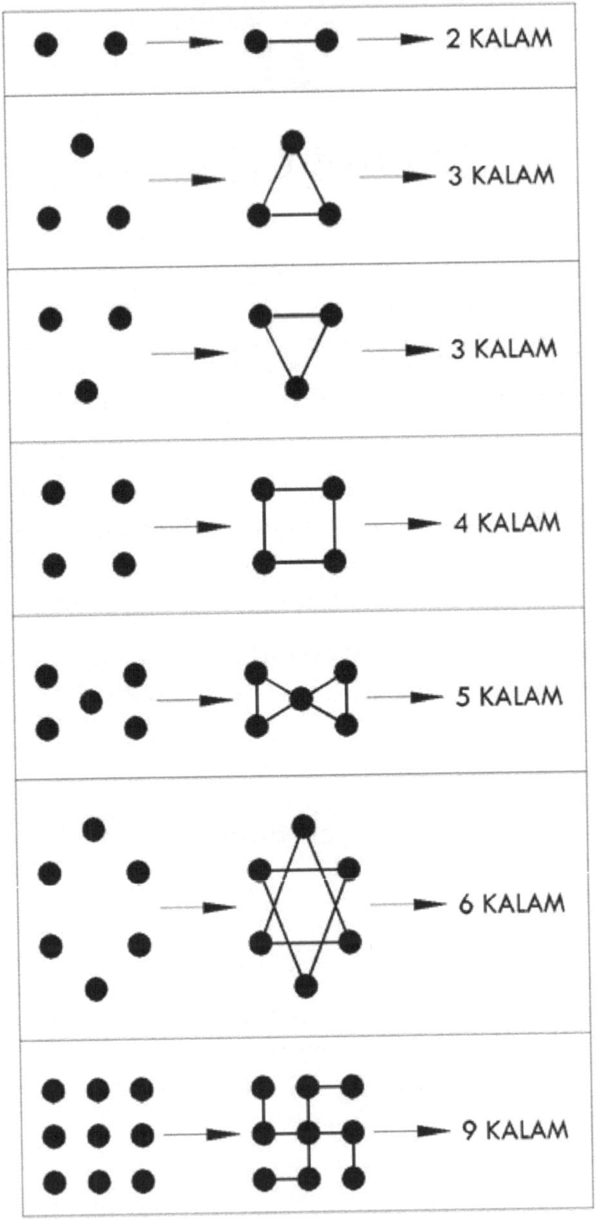

Figure: *A few geometric patterns used in practice of Kalam Chavitt*

Figure: *A maestro of Kalam Chavitt sampradayam Shri. Ashraf Gurukkal*

All patterns are mostly a combination of these geometric figures.

The principles adopted are very different from those of other styles of Kalaripayattu, as emphasis is given to staying close to the opponent and finding a strategic position where the opponent's power and size advantage is negated through proper footwork (it is always to be assumed that the opponent is bigger and stronger than you).

Here, asymmetrical strikes or attacks are also given more importance to takedown by any opponent within a short period.

Mei kalam and Mei Chuvadus are used for body conditioning.

Figure: *An eye gouging technique in Kalam Chavitt*

Kalam Chavitt doesn't only mean floor patterns; they also recognize geometry in blocking, attacking, and body alignment during combat.

It shares many similarities with Yantra Chuvadus (patterns based on Hindu Tantra) in various lineages.

It is more of a barehand-oriented system.

Commonly used weapons are bo staff, short stick, dagger, sword and shield, spear, and Urumi.

Weapons are also mostly practiced in definitive footwork patterns.

It is a mystical system that provides much life understanding, too. For example,

> The practice of One Kalam denotes the presence of one universal consciousness or ultimate truth.
>
> Practice of Two Kalam shows the presence of two energies: masculine and feminine (Shiva and Shakti)

Three Kalam represents Tridosha (Vata, Pitta, Kapha), Trigun (Rajas, Tamas, Sattva), and three important Nadis (Ida, Pingala, Sushumna)

Four Kalam stands for four pillars of human life: Mata, Pita, Guru, and Daiva (Mother, Father, Teacher, and the God).

Five Kalam explains the interconnection of Pancha Mahabhuta (five elements), Panchaindriya (five senses), and Panchavayu (five important Vayus).

Likewise, the same yogic and spiritual interpretation can be given till 64 Kalam.

The footwork practices of Kalam Chavitt are very similar to those of other Southeastern systems, such as Silat and Kali.

Kalam Chavitt lacks flashy movements and focuses on practical and functional self-defense techniques.

The system's unique feature is that one particular footwork pattern is tested and functionally practiced for all ranges (kicking, punching, elbowing, and grappling ranges).

This system focuses mainly on self-defense and survival.

I. Yantra Chuvadus

Yantras are powerful geometric designs used in Hinduism and Tantric Buddhism for meditation, worship, and spiritual transformation. They represent deities and are believed to harness cosmic and spiritual powers. The idea that "mathematics is the language of the Gods" suggests that the consciousness of God is expressed through intricate patterns of mathematics and geometry. Dr. Michio Kaku, a prominent theoretical physicist, has proposed the idea that we can think of God as a master mathematician. On a cosmic scale, there exists a profound connection between mathematics, sound, and form. In the practice of tantra, the geometric form that symbolizes a particular sound (mantra) is referred to as a yantra. Each pitch and vibration generates a unique, intricate geometric pattern corresponding to its specific frequency. Furthermore, each variation in geometry is linked to a distinct note, pitch, and frequency. The sacred geometric form (yantra) and the celestial sound (mantra) are inseparable, forming the essence of tantra. This gives rise to the profound aphorism "yantra plus mantra equals tantra."

Yantra Chuvadus encompass footwork patterns based on divine yantras, serving as the foundation for both body conditioning and combat techniques with barehand forms or weaponry. This traditional practice is upheld by only a few lineages. It involves the chanting of mantras alongside the practice of footwork patterns based on various yantras. Some lineages specifically focus on the yantra of Sri Chakra, a sacred geometric diagram used in the Shri Vidya school of Hinduism for worship, meditation, and devotion. It consists of nine interlocking triangles, with four upward triangles representing Shiva (masculine) and five downward triangles representing Shakti (feminine). Practitioners learn various footwork techniques on a triangle and then try to consolidate them into a complex and difficult single form.

Figure: *Representation of Sri Yantra*

Similarly, the Swastik Yantra is a composite of squares. After mastering different variations of square footwork, practitioners can combine them to form a Swastik Yantra. By practicing these yantras with a guru-given mantra, students can experience spiritual growth.

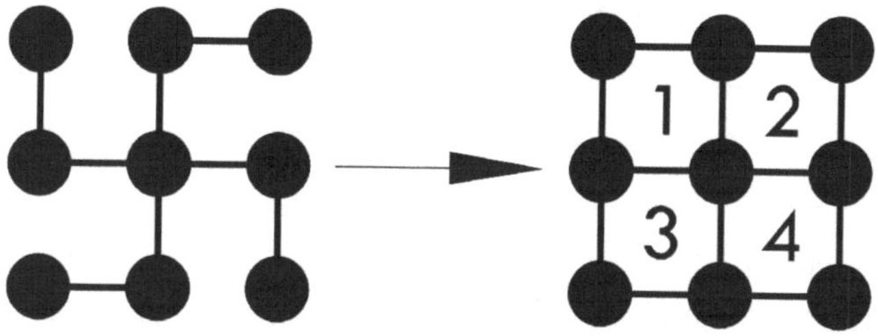

Figure: *Footwork related to swastik yantra learnt as a combination of squares*

Another way of understanding the Yantra Chuvadu is through the concept of 'KONANILA'. Energy flows in our body from marma to marma in specific angular connections, taking various geometric shapes in different parts of the body. This concept or theory is called Konanila. The interrelationship of the Shiva Panchakshara (NA MA SHI VA YA), the five elements that constitute the microcosm and macrocosm, and the concept of Konanila lead to the formation of Yantra Chuvadus representing the geometric patterns and angular connections of energy formed within the body.

Yantra Chuvadus employ precise combat geometry, imparting knowledge of body alignment and placement during combat scenarios. Integrating physical combat with yantra and mantra sadhana enables students to comprehend both the divine and destructive (combat) facets of the art. Yantra Chuvadus are predominantly practiced in the southern style of Kalaripayattu and have strong ties to the Tamil lineage of martial arts.

22

LESSER-KNOWN STYLES OF KALARIPAYATTU

The rural pockets of Kerala, coastal Karnataka, and the Kanyakumari region of Tamil Nadu house a few lesser-known and unique styles of Kalaripayattu.

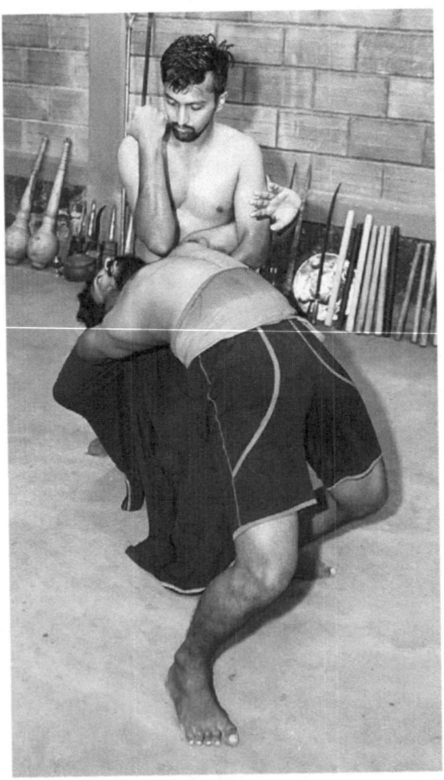

Figure 24. a

Figure 24. b

Figures 24. a–24. b.: *Basic locking techniques in Kalaripayattu*

All these styles add to the system's beauty and diversity. Hanuman Angam, Balivazhy, Garuda Vela, Thulunadan Kalaripayattu, Karnatic Kalaripayattu, and Lahala Mura are a few lineages that can be mentioned under this category.

Each style has its principles and story of origin. For example,

Hanuman Angam is a style built upon the moves inspired from the Hindu god Hanuman.

They also carry a mystical dimension because of their tantra and mantra sadhana with the physical practice.

Tribal styles or Adivasi mura, where Mahabharata characters inspire its moves, can also be seen. If a practitioner moves forward to be offensive, it is called 'Bheemanvazhy,' and if he moves back as an evasion to an attack, it is called 'Panchali mura.' The names of the moves are inspired from Mahabharata characters Bheema and Draupadi. Bheema represents masculinity (offensively moving forward) and Draupadi represents feminine energy (e.g., evading and moving back). Only a few lineages have styles and terms like this, predominantly focusing on barehanded techniques.

I. Hanuman Angam

Hanuman Angam is a mystical sub-style of Kalaripayattu that focuses predominantly on barehanded techniques and spiritual practices.

Figure: *Jinu Aashan of Hanuman Angam*

In the words of Jinu Aashan, a disciple of Ajay Gurukkal (Panthalam, Perumpulikal) and Subash Gurukkal (Adoor, Chendamangalam), Hanuman Angam consists of 6 Chuvadus (forms), 6 Adi Vela, and 18 Margams within each Chuvadu (18 Margams × 6 Chuvadus: 108 Margangal [108 inner techniques]).

A Margam (set of techniques) consists of 6 Chuvadu Muras (inner techniques within a form), 6 Kai (hand) Mura, and 6 Mel Vela.

Each Chuvadu has 6 Ozhivu margam (evasive techniques).

The first Chuvadu among the six Chuvadus will teach the practitioner to counter an attack from the front direction.

The Second Chuvadu aids the practitioner in learning to retaliate to attacks from the back.

The third and the fourth Chuvadu are used to counter attacks from the practitioner's left- and right-hand sides.

The fifth Chuvadu involves 'Kandam Mari' (360° turn), and the sixth Chuvadu involves offensive and defensive movements with legs.

The practices of Hanuman Angam can also be divided into Keezhangam and Melangam.

Practitioners of this style are said to gain the strength and blessings of Lord Hanuman through physical and spiritual practices.

In this style, all pujas are dedicated to Lord Hanuman.

A student is initiated by the Guru into the class through a puja on an auspicious day.

Then, the student has to do 12 pujas with a 21-day gap between each puja.

Then, the practitioner is introduced into weaponry through a ritual done seven days before an Amavasya (the lunar phase of the new moon).

The practitioner again starts the next level of spiritual sadhana from the Amavasya and continues it for the next 21 Amavasyas.

The student will accompany his or her spiritual sadhana with physical practice during this period.

Maintaining a strict diet and celibacy is a must.

After the 21 Amavasyas, the student is given a stick, a knife and a garland as a symbol of accomplishment of a level by the Guru.

Velas or techniques within the style are hard for a nonpractitioner to decipher.

The style is said to have a strong connection with Tamil martial arts, as its roots can be traced to Kanyakumari.

II. Katina Yoga

Katina yoga is a mystical sub-style of Kalaripayattu.

Kalari Vidya can be bifurcated into two sects as Sarala yoga and Katina yoga.

Figure: *Kishore gurukkal demonstrating a movement in Katina yoga*

Sarala yoga involves eye-pleasing, performance-oriented movements that are easy to learn.

Katina yoga involves practical, effective fighting techniques that are hard to learn and not so eye-pleasing.

Katina yoga can be divided into following three categories:

1. Adhi Bhautikam
2. Adhi Daivikam
3. Adyatmikam

Adhi Bhautikam involves body-conditioning exercises.

Initially, the student is introduced to Kalari and Guru Vanakkam (salutation forms), Kalari Nila (stance), Panchakshara Pranayama, Surya Namaskara, and Kachakettal.

Then, 32 basic Chuvadus (Angam, MunAngam, Mukoonam, Nalu Konam, Dasha Konam, Chakra Samharam, etc.) are taught, with 96 associated perukka Chuvadus.

The next level of the syllabus involves various Pidi Mura (locking techniques), Puliyangam (fighting tactics of the tiger), Chadakkam (animal movements), and Bali Mura.

Then comes more advanced Chuvadus like Akshara Kalam, Mantra Kalam, and Nakshatra Kalam, which aid in activating the Nadis and 51 Aksharas, or sounds, in the human body.

Then, the student is taught eight types of perukkam that improve the *prana bala* (strength of vital force).

Adhi Daivikam involves the study of Parapara Tattvas, Jeevan, Prana Vayu, Marmas, and the 96 Tattvas. Students learn how to attack various Marmas and heal them through various Adangals (massage techniques).

Channelising the Prana Shakti is also given importance through various *kriyas*.

Adhyatmikam involves practices of Pranayama, Vasi Yoga, Siva Yoga, Sara Yoga, and understanding Amrita Nilai.

Figure: *Sage Shukracharya, also known as Asuracharya or Daitya Guru, was a sage and guru to the asuras (demons) and danavs in ancient India. An ardent devotee of Shiva, Shukracharya is said to have attained the Mitra Sanjeevani Vidya mantra from the god, allowing him to revive anyone from the dead.*

Mantra meditation, like Panchakshara Perukkam, is of great importance here.

Katina yoga aids the practitioner in learning self-defense through spiritual understanding and practices.

Sage Shukracharya is said to be the acharya or guru of Katina yoga, and Bhagavad Shukracharya Samhita is its main source text.

23

UNDERSTANDING KALARIPAYATTU THROUGH SANATANA DHARMA

Sanatana Dharma is foundational to the cultural identity of Bharat. The two great epics of this land, the Ramayana and the Mahabharata, illustrate how weapons were used to uphold Dharma (righteousness) over Adharma (evil). Sanatana Dharma holds both Nirguna Parabrahma (formless, eternal consciousness) and the Saguna (embodied) form of worship. Nirguna Parabrahma takes Saguna forms of Shiva (masculine energy) and Shakti (feminine energy). In this view, Shiva is revered as the father, while Shakti, in the form of Maa Durga, is honored as the mother of Kalaripayattu, symbolizing both protection and origin.

Shiva is said to have imparted the knowledge of Kalaripayattu to Parashurama (the sixth avatar of Vishnu). Vishnu's Dashavataras (Ten Incarnations) offer practitioners both physical techniques and deeper spiritual teachings, each avatar embodying principles that Kalaripayattu practitioners can adopt. Lord Rama, known as Maryada Purushottama (the ideal man), exemplifies moral values for a Kalaripayattu practitioner to follow, while Lord Hanuman, his devoted follower, embodies the Bhakti that one should possess. There are flying attacks and unarmed techniques in Kalaripayattu inspired from Hanuman's strength and agility. Lord Krishna imparts lessons on diplomacy, tactfulness, and

Figure: *Vishwaroopam of the Supreme Being*

intelligence in conflict. Certain lineages incorporate combat applications inspired from Krishna's cross-legged stance, and it is believed that open-hand strikes in Kalaripayattu may have been inspired from Krishna's Narayani Sena, who were considered experts in such techniques.

The Dashavatara also inspire Vadivus in Kalaripayattu, such as Varaha (wild boar), Simha (lion), and Matsya (fish), reflecting the Varaha, Narasimha, and Matsya avatars of Vishnu. Vishnu's avatars, Rama and Krishna, are the leads of the Ramayana and Mahabharata, both of which depict significant conflict to uphold Dharma. Thus, Vishnu represents the spirit of Kalaripayattu, using force when necessary to uphold righteousness.

The tradition also reveres Shiva's son, Ganapathy, who embodies the strength a Kalaripayattu student should cultivate. The divine weapon Otta, used in Kalaripayattu, is associated with him. Another son of Shiva, Karthikeya (or Skanda), the Suraloka Nathan (chief of the divine army), represents bravery and leadership. His vehicle, the Mayura (peacock), and his flag emblem, the Kukkuda (rooster), are significant Vadivus in Kalaripayattu. Karthikeya is believed to have shared his martial wisdom with Sage Agasthya, who is regarded as the founder of the Tamil lineage of martial systems and is connected to the Southern style of Kalaripayattu. In Silambam (the Tamil bo staff fighting system), the staff is said to represent Lord Murugan's (Karthikeya) weapon, the Vel. Lord Ayyappa is also revered as a practitioner of Kalaripayattu.The serpent around Shiva's neck, symbolizing Kundalini Shakti, has inspired several combative techniques that reflect the snake's movement and striking behavior.

Kalaripayattu draws its ethical code, values, and combat nuances from Sanatana Dharma, which serves as a spiritual foundation for practitioners. However, it is understood that not all practitioners necessarily see Kalaripayattu through this spiritual lens. Kalaripayattu's inclusive tradition encourages students to approach the art in a way that resonates with their beliefs. Ultimately, all Kalaripayattu practitioners share a dedication to humanity, justice, and righteousness in society.

I. Relating Bhagavad Gita and Kalaripayattu

Kalaripayattu traces its origins to Parashurama, an avatar of Vishnu. Similarly, the Bhagavad Gita, the sacred dialogue on dharma, was delivered by another avatar, Vasudeva Krishna. Both Kalaripayattu and the Bhagavad Gita have strong ties to the epic Mahabharata, and each has played a pivotal role in shaping the warrior spirit and the quest for dharma (righteousness) in Indian culture.

The Gita unfolds on the battlefield of Kurukshetra as Krishna imparts divine wisdom to Arjuna, who stands uncertain before the impending Mahabharata war. Similarly, Kalaripayattu is not only a martial art but also a battlefield discipline, a means of defending dharma. Many Kalaripayattu techniques are inspired from characters from the Mahabharata, including Krishna himself. Arjuna's chariot bears the emblem of Lord Hanuman, revered for his strength, skill, and loyalty—qualities Kalaripayattu practitioners seek to embody.

The Bhagavad Gita guides readers toward an understanding of dharma, encouraging them to rise beyond personal doubts and act with selflessness and integrity. Far from being a call to pacifism, the Gita provides insight into kshatra dharma, the warrior's code of duty and honor. When studied alongside the physical discipline of Kalaripayattu, the Gita's teachings become a powerful tool for the next generation, instilling clarity, peace, and commitment to higher values.

Both Kalaripayattu and the Bhagavad Gita emphasize themes of duty, self-mastery, mindfulness, and spiritual evolution. Together, they bridge physical skill and spiritual wisdom, preparing practitioners to act with poise, presence, and adherence to a greater purpose. Kalaripayattu also incorporates mantra sadhana, or the repetition of sacred chants, which aligns with the revered Vishnu Sahasranama—a thousand names of

Vishnu recited by Gangaputra Bhishma on the same battlefield of Kurukshetra in the presence of Lord Krishna.

In essence, the combined practice of Kalaripayattu, the Vishnu Sahasranama, and the wisdom of the Bhagavad Gita offers a holistic path to self-realization. This trio provides a blueprint for living in harmony with dharma, empowering individuals to cultivate inner strength, resilience, and a profound sense of purpose.

II. Relating the Divine Weapons in Sanatana Dharma and Kalaripayattu

Trishula (Trident)

The trident is a powerful weapon associated with both Shiva and Shakti (Maa Durga). It serves as a source of inspiration for footwork patterns (Chuvadu forms) and striking hand gestures (Kai mudras) within various lineages of Kalaripayattu. Spiritually, the Trishula embodies the divine balance of creation, preservation, and destruction.

Figure: *Represention of Goddess Durga with various weapons*

Chakra (Wheel)

The Sudarshana Chakra, wielded by Lord Vishnu, is connected to circular footwork and the rotational torque generated by the body during combat. Maa Durga also carries a chakra, gifted by Vishnu, for the annihilation of the demon Mahishasura. In Kalaripayattu, the Chakra Mudra is employed as an attacking hand gesture.

Gada (Mace)

Classified as a wooden weapon in Kalaripayattu, the Gada is primarily associated with the Hindu God Hanuman. Lord Vishnu also wields a gada named '*Kaumodaki*'. Notable characters from the Mahabharata, such as Bhima, Balarama, and Duryodhana, were masters of Gada-Yuddha (mace combat).

Spear (Vel)

The Vel, representing a long stick or Kuntham in Kalaripayattu, is the weapon of Lord Muruga (Karthikeya). It is said that Agni Dev, the God of Fire, bestowed a spear upon Maa Durga. This weapon symbolizes fiery power and the ability to discern right from wrong, reflecting the Goddess's unwavering commitment to righteousness.

Khadga (Sword)

The sword holds significant cultural and historical importance in Kalaripayattu. Lord Vishnu has a sword named '*Nandaki*,' and a sword was given to Maa Durga by Lord Ganesh. The blade of the sword represents the brilliance of knowledge, while its sharpness signifies wisdom, illustrating the synergy of understanding and intellect that prevails over negativity.

Parashu (Axe)

In Kalaripayattu, the axe is referred to as Venmazhu. It is the weapon of Lord Parashurama. Lord Shiva gave his axe, Parashu, to Parashurama, and taught him how to use it. The axe was named '*Vidyudabhi*'. Lord Vishwakarma, the divine architect, provided an axe to Maa Durga. This weapon symbolizes fearlessness in adversity, embodying the dual power to destroy and create, empowering the Goddess to confront evil without hesitation.

Dhanurvidya (Archery)

Certain lineages of Kalaripayattu include the Bow and Arrow (Dhanurvidya) in their training. Lord Vishnu possesses a bow named '*Sharanga,*' while Vayu Dev, the God of Air, granted Durga her Bow and Arrow. The arrow signifies swift action, while the bow represents focus and potential, epitomizing the balance of power and possibility within us all.

Notable Bows and Arrows in Hindu Puranas:

Pinaka: Lord Shiva's simple yet unbreakable bow.

Gandiva: The bow of Arjuna, gifted by Agni, the fire god.

Kodanda: Lord Rama's bow, integral to his warrior persona in the Ramayana.

Vijaya: The renowned bow of Karna, famed for its indestructibility.

Pulsatya: Ravana's bow, highlighting his exceptional archery skills.

Pratignya: The bow of Bhishma, a legendary warrior in the Mahabharata.

Kamadeva's Bow: Made of sugarcane, it shoots arrows of flowers, embodying love and beauty.

Shanka (Conch)

In Hindu Puranas, the conch, or 'shankha,' symbolizes creation and is closely linked to the preserver god Vishnu. Lord Vishnu's shankha, known as '*Panchajanya*,' is often depicted in his right hand as a divine weapon capable of creation, protection, and destruction. It resonates with the primordial sound of "Om," the essence of creation, and embodies the Vedic concept of Prana, the universal life force. In Kalaripayattu, the 'Shanka Mudra' is a Kai mudra used for attack.

Sarpam (Snake)

Maa Durga is depicted holding a snake in one of her hands, which is also integrated into Kalaripayattu as a Vadivu. The snake symbolizes consciousness and the transformative male energy of Lord Shiva, representing the evolution from a lower to a higher state of awareness. It embodies Kundalini Shakti, the primal energy that drives personal and spiritual growth.

III. Shiva and Kalaripayattu

Shiva! He is a cosmic force, a divine phenomenon; he is both nothingness and everythingness.

For the followers of the principles of Sanatana Dharma, Shiva is the source of Music (Damaru), Dance (Tandava) and Combat (Trishula).

Be it the lineage of Parashurama (Northern style of Kalaripayattu) or Agasthya (Southern style of Kalaripayattu), the root of the knowledge is Shiva himself.

His divine weapon - Trishula, the three prongs depicting the past, present, and future - represents his combative essence.

Figure: *Trishula footwork pattern*

Shiva's Trishula has been Dharma's eternal guardian in the past. It is the guardian now and will protect Dharma in the future, too.

South Indian combat systems have an attacking Kai Mudra (hand gesture) and footwork (Chuvadu) related to Trishula.

In the Vigyana Bhairava tantra, Shiva tells his consort, Parvati, that she is also part of Shiva and that they are not two separate entities.

Hanuman Chalisa mentions "Shankar Swayam Kesari Nandan" Meaning to say Lord Hanuman (son of Kesari) is Shiva himself.

It is also said "Sivasya Hridayam Vishnur - Vishnoshcha Hridayam Sivah," meaning Shiva is the heart of Vishnu and Vishnu is the heart of Shiva.

In the Krishna Yajur Veda, Skanda Upanishad, Shiva and Vishnu are said to be the same entity. They are different names given to the supreme consciousness.

Lord Ganesha, Karthikeya, and Ayyappa are branches of one big tree named Shiva.

So, the animal's postures and forms, recognizing themselves with any particular deity, will ultimately connect to Shiva.

The Sacred Panchakshara *NA-MA-SHI-VA-YA* are connected to the five elements.

Five elements connect themselves to the five senses.

Elements, senses, and the five Vayus connect themselves to Chakras.

Chakras and Nadis lead the way to knowledge of Marmas.

Figure: *Nataraja Vadivu (Pose inspired from Tandava posture of Shiva)*

So, understanding the Shiva Panchakshara will open up a new dimension of knowledge for the practitioner of Kalaripayattu.

Shiva Tandava Chuvadu (forms related to Shiva's cosmic dance) is also practiced in a few lineages.

Nataraja Vadivu (posture inspired from the dancing pose of Shiva) is also practiced in a few Kalaris.

The relationship between Shiva and Kalaripayattu is eternal.

According to me, Kalaripayattu is a lifestyle designed to reach the ultimate reality through Kshatra Dharma.

Shivoham!

24

IS KALARIPAYATTU THE MOTHER OF ALL MARTIAL ARTS?

Firstly, it's important to understand that Kalaripayattu is a regional term mainly associated with the Indian state of Kerala and is part of the broader umbrella of martial arts systems originating in southern India. There is always a debate about which combat lineage is older: the Tamil lineage of martial arts (Silambam, Kuthuvarisai, Varmakalai, etc.) or Kalaripayattu. Putting that debate aside and examining the martial systems

Figure 25.a: *Bodhidharma*

of southern India in a unified manner can help answer many questions.

There's a popular belief that Bodhidharma, a Tamil king, learned the native combat system of South India and then went to China to establish the Shaolin temple. However, concrete proof is needed for this claim. It's worth noting that China had experience with warfare before Bodhidharma's arrival. Bodhidharma is said to have contributed bone marrow cleansing and other yogic breathing techniques to the prevailing martial practices of China. It's also known that the Indian monk Buddhabhadra (BaTuo) preceded Bodidharma in reaching China and became the first Abbott of the Shaolin Monastery.

The combat systems of southern India have influenced Chinese martial systems, much like the teachings of Buddhism and trade.

Okinawan martial arts like Karate, Megumi, and kobudō were influenced by Japan, China, and Southeast Asia due to Okinawa's location. Chinese Kung fu was influenced by Indian combat systems and, in turn, influenced arts like Karate, suggesting potential links between Indian and Okinawan martial practices.

Other well-known Southeastern fighting styles in Thailand (Muay Boran, Muay Thai, etc.) and Cambodia (Bokator) have strong cultural ties to the Indian epic Ramayana. The flying strikes of Hanuman and related stories illustrate the Indian influence.

Filipino martial arts, commonly known as Kali, also have close connections with Indian martial systems. The forward triangle footwork in Kali is also referred to as male triangle footwork. This figure in Indian Tantra and martial systems is called Shiva (masculine energy). The reverse triangle, or the female triangle of Kali, is called Shakti (feminine energy) in India (Refer to figure 25 b). Shamanic practices, medicinal systems, and the Guro language of the Philippines have an Indian influence. Sri Lankan Angampora is closely related to the Kanyakumari style of martial arts. Kanyakumari, referred as "The Land's End", is the southernmost tip of the Indian subcontinent and the southernmost city in mainland India.

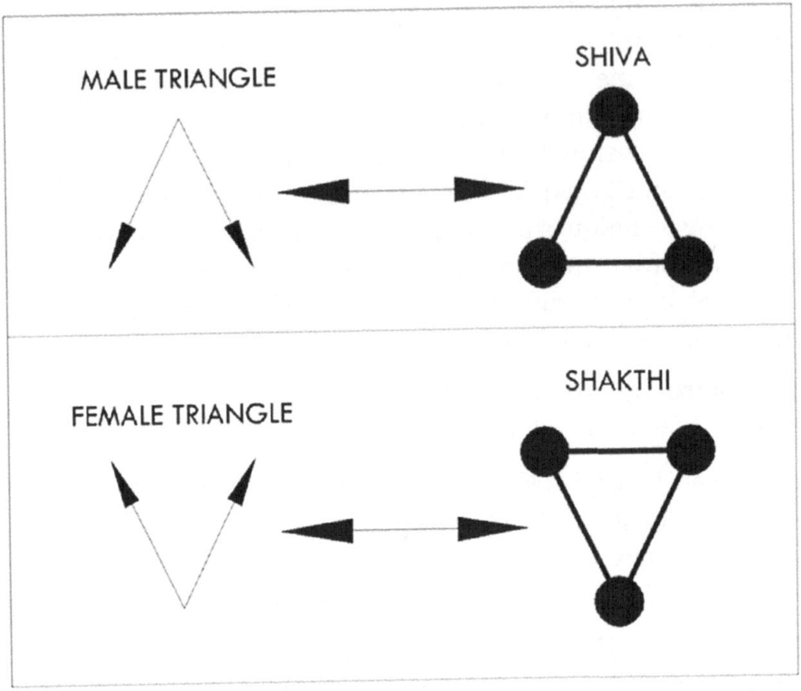

Figure 25.b: *Similarity in interpretation of the triangle in in Filipino martial arts and Indian martial systems*

Footwork patterns in Indonesian and Malaysian art of Silat are similar to those used in Kalam Chavitt Kalaripayattu and Tamil martial arts.

The Indian connection with native European, American and African combat systems needs further research.

The influence of Indian martial systems on combat systems of other nations is undeniable. Is Kalaripayattu the mother? Probably not, as the Tamil combat systems have also influenced the martial practices of other countries equally. However, Kalaripayattu can be regarded as the mother of martial arts from two perspectives. The first view holds that Shiva is the origin of combat, with both the lineages of Parashurama and Agasthya identifying him as the Adi Guru (the first teacher). This combat system, blessed by Shiva and Shakti (Durga) and connected to Dhanurveda, is believed to be the root of all martial arts from this standpoint. The second perspective sees Kalaripayattu as an ancient spiritual and physical discipline encompassing not only all aspects of unarmed combat but also a wide array of weaponry in all possible fighting ranges. These techniques and weapon disciplines are holistically integrated within Kalaripayattu, reflecting practices found in martial arts traditions worldwide. This suggests that its influence may have spread widely, laying the foundation for various fighting systems across cultures.

25

OTHER INDIAN COMBAT STYLES

India has a rich history of warfare dating back to the times of Ramayana and Mahabharata. Like Kalaripayattu in southern India, different regions of the country have their own distinct martial art traditions.

To name a few:

1. *Gatka*: Punjab
2. *Silambam*: Tamil Nadu
3. *Kuthuvarisai*: Tamil Nadu
4. *Varmakalai*: Tamil Nadu
5. *Mardhani Khel*: Maharashtra
6. *Thang Ta*: Manipur
7. *Sarik Sarak*: Manipur
8. *Inbuan Wrestling*: Mizoram
9. *Lathi*: West Bengal
10. *Huiyen Llaong*: Manipur
11. *Kushti/Mallayudha*: One can see traces all over the country

26

PERFORMING ARTS RELATED TO KALARIPAYATTU

Many performing arts in Kerala incorporate the weapons and movements of Kalaripayattu.

Figure: *Kathakali*

Kathakali (the classical dance drama of Kerala), *Theyyam* (an artistic performance done at temples and its participants dress up and pretend to be the gods and goddesses of the hosting temple), *Onathallum Kaiporum* (hand fighting festival), *Yathrakali* (also called Sangakali an art reserved to be performed only by Brahmins), *Krishnanatam, Kolkali* (the short stick from Kalaripayattu is used in Kolkali, often in fast-paced routines with dancers holding a stick in each hand), *Parija Muthukali, Chavittunadakam* (a Christian art based on Kalaripayattu) and tribal dances are a few examples of such arts.

Figure: *Theyyam performers performing with sword and shield*

27

KALARIPAYATTU AS A SPORT

The modern world's evolving landscape of martial arts encompasses three distinct variations: traditional combat practices, demonstration, and sports. Kalaripayattu is also navigating through these different dimensions.

The Government of India has officially recognized Kalaripayattu as a sport for prestigious events such as the Khelo India Games and the National Games. This recognition allows practitioners to excel in their chosen fields by earning medals, advancing their academic pursuits, or securing employment prospects.

However, certain concerns have surfaced amidst this progress. With an incessant series of championships and a fixed syllabus, there is a risk that students may prioritize winning medals over the authentic practice and essence of Kalari. This emphasis on competition-specific forms may produce adept performers, yet it may overlook the development of true warriors.

One significant consideration is preserving the integrity of Kalaripayattu as a combat system beyond its status as a sport. There is a risk that the proliferation of competition-focused syllabi may dilute the authentic essence of the art, diverting practitioners' attention from the rigorous and transformative journey of Kalari practice. The emphasis on winning medals may overshadow the profound psycho-physical impact that sincere engagement with Kalari can impart.

While Kalaripayattu's sports-oriented evolution brings material benefits, it is crucial to ensure that these advancements do not compromise the system's core principles. Achieving a harmonious balance between sports and traditional practice presents a noteworthy challenge. The perennial nature of championships may incline students to prioritize memorizing sequences over understanding their functional application.

Ultimately, the responsibility lies with the community of Kalaripayattu teachers to uphold ethical standards and safeguard the intrinsic soul of this ancient martial art.

As there is a chance of favoritism and nepotism in these events, it is the responsibility of the masters and gurus to make sure the system is non-corrupt and the authenticity is maintained.

In events such as high ball kick, even a non-Kalaripayattu practitioner can compete and get a medal, so stringent rules should be applied to see to it that deserving Kalaripayattu practitioners reap the benefits of the competitions.

While the sports version undoubtedly holds merit, it is imperative to recognize that Kalaripayattu transcends mere accolades and external validation, manifesting as a quintessential lifestyle encompassing profound physical, mental, and spiritual dimensions.

28

REPOSITIONING KALARIPAYATTU IN THE CONTEMPORARY WORLD

Kalaripayattu is an ancient combat system built on strong moral values.

Diluting and limiting it to be a demonstration activity will kill the warrior soul of Kalaripayattu.

When Kalaripayattu is practiced, remembering that it is a combat system will instill in the practitioner the necessary courage, morals, and Kshatra attitude to stand up for what is right in society.

People argue that when Kalari is seen as a fitness activity, it will gain more takers, but when the combat mode of training is lost, it won't remain Kalaripayattu.

For India's law enforcement agencies and national security forces, more scientific and evolved contemporary combat versions of Kalaripayattu should be devised.

This will be the contribution of the Kalari fraternity to 'Make in India' and Atma Nirbhar Bharath Initiatives.

For civilians, the traditional Kalari training and its functional testing to combat modern violence scenarios will create a healthier, more secure, and braver society.

Figure: *A Kalaripayattu retention lock*

Along with the present academic syllabus, students should also be educated about the importance of indigenous systems of combat and medicine.

After learning Kalaripayattu, with its pure moral and combative essence, one can use it for demonstrations or pursue it as a sport.

People also should understand that Kalaripayattu used as a part of dance shows and various other stage performances is just a mere physical representation of movements.

The soul and heart of it lies elsewhere.

The difference between a performing artist and an actual Kalaripayattu warrior should always be understood.

The onus is on the present generation to preserve Kalaripayattu properly and treat its demonstration and sports version as value additions.

A society filled with great physical strength, combat capability, and a calm aura is required to take the human consciousness to the next level.

I. Women's Safety

Kalaripayattu, a martial art deeply rooted in a culture that honors the strength and dignity of women, is guided by principles like:

"Śaktiḥ strīṇāṁ surakṣā yatra, tatra vijayaḥ" ("Where there is strength and security for women, there lies victory") and *"Yatra nāryastu pūjyante, ramante tatra devatāḥ"* ("Where women are honored, there the divine resides").

In a world where violence against women—such as rape, harassment, abuse, and assault—remains prevalent, Kalaripayattu offers more than physical training. It empowers women with self-confidence and effective self-defense skills. Within Indian culture, the mother is revered as a child's first teacher. When a mother or sister is skilled in Kalaripayattu, she can protect herself and cultivate resilience in her family, inspiring future generations to embody strength and self-assurance.

Kalaripayattu instructors play a vital role in expanding access for women through workshops and seminars that showcase the art's transformative benefits. By combining practical combat techniques across Kalaripayattu styles, specialized self-defense courses can be developed to equip women with strategies to face real-world threats.

Women embody both the grace of Mahalakshmi and the fierce strength of Mahakali. Indigenous martial arts of India help them awaken this inner Kali, fostering physical power, mental clarity, and self-reliance. These practices reconnect women with their innate capacity to nurture and protect, embodying a powerful duality.

Kalaripayattu celebrates the divine feminine, particularly in the form of Maa Durga. As the saying goes, "*Nārī śakti rūpeṇa sansthita*"—a woman embodies the essence of strength. By embracing Kalaripayattu, women not only enhance their own safety but also contribute to a society that honors feminine power, fostering a resilient and empowered community.

29

BENEFITS OF LEARNING KALARIPAYATTU

In Kalaripayattu, each movement comprises three essential dimensions: body conditioning, combat interpretation, and spiritual knowledge to enrich our lives. Through rigorous body conditioning, Kalaripayattu enables practitioners to attain balanced Tridosha, enhance Prana Shakti, gain improved control over the mind, boost immunity, and achieve heightened physical and mental flexibility, resulting in great self-confidence. Combat training empowers us to skilfully confront any potential threat with efficiency.

Spiritually, it offers profound benefits to practitioners. When practiced correctly, Kalaripayattu instills the morals of Lord Rama, the tactfulness and diplomacy of Lord Krishna, the Bhakti of Lord Hanuman, the courage of Lord Murugan, and spiritual charm from the Hari-Hara-Shakti trio (Shiva-Vishnu-Durga). According to the "Kalaripayattu Prayer," consistent practice bestows upon practitioners six essential qualities: strength, patience, righteousness, lightning speed in movement and decision-making, the fury of Goddess Kali, and commanding power.

"Kalari Sadhanam Klesha Samharam"

The consistent practice of Kalaripayattu (Kalari Sadhanam) will exterminate (SAMHARAM) all the toxins (KLESHAS) that afflict a human being.

I. When the Body Becomes All Eyes

This line or phrase describes the ideal state of accomplishment of a Kalaripayattu practitioner when in combat. In Malayalam, it is called "*Meyyu Kannakuka*".

When the practitioner reaches this state, he will be potent enough to respond to any attack from any direction or stimulus in his environment.

The line refers to an extreme form of concentration in which the level of alertness lifts the practitioner to a higher state of being.

II. The Real Purpose of Kalaripayattu

In the modern world, Kalaripayattu is frequently reduced to a fitness routine or a form of cultural demonstration. Although it is often regarded as a means for physical conditioning or an artistic expression of heritage, Kalaripayattu is much more than a set of techniques for self-defense or a display of skill. This ancient Indian martial art embodies profound spiritual, ethical, and philosophical dimensions that transcend its physical aspects.

Why, then, should one commit to practicing Kalaripayattu? The answer lies not only in its benefits for health, patriotism, or self-defense, but in its potential to elevate the practitioner's mind and spirit. Kalaripayattu teaches that the practitioner and the weapon must be unified, with the weapon becoming an extension of one's own body. This principle of unity is not merely for combat—it is a symbolic and preparatory step toward achieving harmony with nature, with society, and ultimately, with the universal consciousness. The mastery of weapon and body, guided by discipline and respect, fosters a deeper connection to the world around us.

The roots of Kalaripayattu are firmly embedded in Sanatana Dharma, an ancient and eternal framework of values and virtues. Dharma, which means righteousness, serves as a guiding principle of Sanatana Dharma and represents a universal moral code. Through scriptures like the Vedas, the Bhagavad Gita, and the Shiva Sutras, Sanatana Dharma provides a comprehensive guide to right action, just living, and the principles of truth and justice. When the righteousness of society is at risk—whether through injustice, corruption, or violence—systems like Kalaripayattu serve as powerful tools to uphold Dharma and to defend moral integrity.

It is crucial to understand that Dharma, in this context, does not imply religion. Here, Dharma is synonymous with righteousness and moral order, extending far beyond the boundaries of personal belief. Kalaripayattu cultivates this understanding within each practitioner, encouraging them to internalize Dharma as an individual and collective responsibility. It teaches that the true warrior, or Kshatriya, is one who protects the values of goodness and justice, ready to act when the moral balance of society is disrupted. This is the essence of Kshatra Dharma—the warrior's duty to defend righteousness, to shield society from harm, and to stand unwavering in the face of adversity.

Kalaripayattu's ultimate purpose is to cultivate not only a warrior but a guardian of Dharma. Through disciplined practice, it builds physical health, mental resilience, and moral clarity, preparing the practitioner to protect righteousness both in personal life and within society. By mastering Kalaripayattu, one gains the strength to confront not only external threats but also inner challenges, embodying the values of truth, justice, and integrity

To practice Kalaripayattu is to embrace a path that aligns body, mind, and spirit with Dharma itself—righteous, vigilant, and committed to defending the greater good.

30

WHY SHOULD ONE LEARN SELF-DEFENSE?

Martial arts, such as Kalaripayattu, offer far more than physical training—they are transformative practices for both body and mind. These ancient arts not only enhance physical fitness and mental resilience but also equip practitioners with the skills to protect themselves and others in dangerous situations.

Unlike many other responsibilities that can be entrusted to specialists—like consulting a doctor for an illness or hiring an architect to design a home—self-defense demands an immediate, personal response. When faced with an unexpected attack, there's no time to rely on others; your ability to react decisively could make all the difference.

This is where the practice of Kalaripayattu shines. It prepares you physically and spiritually, fostering self-confidence and a readiness to handle adversity. A single unfortunate encounter can have life-altering consequences for you and your loved ones, highlighting the importance of self-defense as a proactive skill.

Moreover, by embracing Kalaripayattu, we connect with Bharat's rich legacy of Kshatra Dharma—the warrior spirit that embodies courage, honor, and self-discipline. Becoming a true Kshatriya (warrior) is not a matter of birth but of cultivating strength, principles, and mastery through practices like Shastra Sadhana (martial training).

In the contemporary world, the essence of Lord Krishna reminds us that wielding the "Sudarshana Chakra" is just as essential as holding the "flute." While the flute embodies peace and compassion, the Sudarshana Chakra stands for strength and protection—both are crucial today. Reclaiming Kshatra Dharma through combat training is not merely a choice but a necessity to protect ourselves and our society. By cultivating these qualities, we actively build a community grounded in morality and courage, equipped to face the challenges of our time.

GLOSSARY

Aasan: *Teacher.*

Adangal: *A process in Siddha medicine that involves retrieving affected varma points in the body.*

Adavu: *The basic 'forms' or levels of kalari training.*

Agasthya: *A sage who became well-versed in the Vedas and a variety of sciences, renowned for his use of many weapons. Practitioners of the Southern style of Kalaripayattu and Silambam claim their lineage of martial, medical, and meditation practice from Agasthya, who is believed to be doing penance in the Agasthyakoota hills (Kanyakumari district, Tamil Nadu).*

Asana: *Basic forms or postures of hatha yoga, similar to poses (vadivu) in martial practice.*

Ayurveda: *Indigenous Indian medical system traced from the Vedas.*

Balivazhy: *A substyle of Kalaripayattu based on the Ramayana character BALI, the king of Kishkinda.*

Bhava: *Refers to the inner form or state of mind during practice.*

Chakra: *Energy centers or wheels present in the subtle body.*

Chattankal: *Jumps or leaps.*

Cheruvadi: *A short stick.*

Chottachan: *Small stick, often rounded at both ends, concealed in the hand, and used to attack the body's vital spots.*

Chummuttadi: *Self-defense sequences combining poses, steps, kicks, and hits, usually associated with the 'central' and 'northern' styles of Kalaripayattu practice.*

Chuvadu: *Footwork or steps in Kalaripayattu practice.*

Dakshina: *Traditional 'gifts' or 'offerings' a student gives to their teacher at the beginning and end of a course of training.*

Dhanur Veda: *The 'science of the bow,' one of the traditional eighteen branches of knowledge. Kalaripayattu traces its ancestry to Dhanur Veda.*

Dharma: *The eternal and inherent nature of reality, regarded in Hinduism as a cosmic law underlying proper behavior and social order.*

Gadha: *Mace.*

Gurukkal: *Plural of 'guru,' referring to one's teacher, the teacher's teachers, and the lineage of practice. A term of respect in Kalaripayattu.*

Gurutvam: *Complete trust in one's master.*

Jeevatma: *Individual consciousness.*

Kaalugal: *Leg raises in Kalaripayattu, a body-conditioning exercise with spiritual and combat interpretations.*

Kacha: *The long cloth wrapped around the abdominal/hip area to support the practitioner's vital energy.*

Kalam: *Cleared space used for training/footwork in Kalari, as well as patterns drawn daily outside homes in southern Kerala.*

Kaikuthipayattu: *A body-conditioning exercise in Kalaripayattu*

Kaithada: *Kalaripayattu drills for practicing hitting and blocking.*

Kathakali: *An Indian classical dance form.*

Kathi: *Knives.*

Katina Yoga: *A style of Kalari formulated by Sage Shukracharya.*

Kattaram: *A double-edged short-range weapon.*

Kathiyum thalayum: *Knives and long cloth.*

Kettukaripayattu: *Long stick fighting in the Northern style of Kalaripayattu.*

Kshatriya: *A member of the governing or ruling order.*

Kuli Kalari: *A traditional 'pit' style Kalari dug out of the ground with a pounded earth floor and palm-leaf roof.*

Kundalini: *It is a form of latent spiritual energy believed to reside at the base of the spine, which, when awakened, ascends through the chakras to bring heightened consciousness and spiritual enlightenment.*

Kuntham: *Spear.*

Mahabharata: *An Indian epic focusing on the conflict between Kauravas and Pandavas, with Lord Krishna as the central figure.*

Marmam: *Vulnerable vital spots in the human body.*

Marmmanidanam: *A Kalaripayattu text on Marmas or vital spots.*

Meipayattu: *Body exercises combining kicks, steps, jumps, and turns, forming the basic training in Kalaripayattu.*

Meyyabhyasam: *Foundation of Kalaripayattu practice, involving control over the body and mind through daily exercise.*

Mudra: *Special hand or full-body configurations used in yoga and martial arts.*

Muhurtham: *An auspicious time in Hinduism, calculated based on the position of stars and planets.*

Nabhi: *Navel.*

Nadi: *Energy pathway in the subtle body.*

Navaratri Mahotsavam: *An annual pan-Indian festival held for nine nights, marking new beginnings and weapon offerings in Kalari.*

Noku Marmam: *Subtle means of attacking the body's vital spots by simply looking.*

Otta: *A curved wooden stick resembling an elephant's tusk, made of tamarind wood.*

Parashurama: *An incarnation of Mahavishnu, known for wielding an axe named Parashu. Practitioners of Northern Kalaripayattu claim descent from him.*

Poothara: *Multi-tiered platform for the guardian deities in Kalari. Prana or Prana Vayu: The breath(s) or wind(s) circulating within the body, also referring to the 'life force.'*

Pranayama: *Special yogic breathing involving inhalation, retention, exhalation, and pause.*

Prayogam: *Practical application of martial exercises for offense or defense.*

Puja: *Worship of Hindu deities through offerings.*

Ramayana: *An epic narrating the trials of Prince Rama, his brother Lakshmana, and his wife Sita.*

Sampradayam: *Traditional lineage of practice or style.*

Shastra: *Literally 'science,' referring to traditional knowledge.*

Sthula Sharira: *The physical body.*

Sukshma Sharira: *The internal subtle body.*

Theyyam: *Traditional ritual performances in northern Kerala honoring local deities and heroes trained in Kalaripayattu.*

Udaval: *Fencing sword.*

Ulicchil: *Massage given with feet, hands, or medicinal herb bags.*

Urumi: *A five-foot-long flexible sword used against mob attacks.*

Vaal: *Sword.*

Vaalum Parichayum: *Sword and shield.*

Vadakkan pattukal: *Northern traditional oral ballads of Kerala.*

Vadivu: *Stances or Postures, which act as the basic building blocks of Kalaripayattu training.*

Vaaythari: *Verbal instructions recited by the master during practice.*

Vel: *Weapon of Lord Murugan.*

Venmazhu: *Axe.*

Verumkai: *'Empty-hand' techniques of martial practice.*

Yantra: *Sacred diagrams used in martial training with mystical significance.*

Yoga: *Indian philosophy teaching paths to realize ultimate reality, including Bhakti yoga, Raja yoga, Jnana yoga, and Karma yoga.*

SPECIAL THANKS

- Col. Kalyani Deshpande, Indian Army
- Karthik Ganesh, Kalari Sadhana Mysuru
- Chamind Erakkil, Kalari Gurukulam, Thozhiyoor, Guruvayoor.
- Binesh Gopi, Kalari Gurukulam, Thozhiyoor, Guruvayoor
- Sachu Shanmugan, Kalari Gurukulam, Thozhiyoor, Guruvayoor
- Prakaash Kumar Gurukkal, Prasarana Kalari academy, Bengaluru.
- Ranjith Sivaraman, Kalari Gurukulam, Thozhiyoor, Guruvayoor
- Anand Krishna M J, Kalari Gurukulam, Thozhiyoor, Guruvayoor
- Arjun Krishna M J, Kalari Gurukulam, Thozhiyoor, Guruvayoor
- Sudarshan Sampath Gurukkal, Bengaluru
- Ramshad, Kalari Gurukulam, Thozhiyoor, Guruvayoor
- Ajith Theruvath Gurukkal, Universal Kalari, Chelembra
- Arundev Gurukkal, Universal Kalari, Chelembra
- Dr Don V Shaju, Jeevadhara Kalari, Alakode
- Jinu Aashan, Hanuman Angam
- Kishore Gurukkal, Katina Yoga

- Shriram V V, Bengaluru
- Subramanya M S, Geologist
- Rajendra B, Kalari Sadhana Mysuru
- Abhishek, Kalari Sadhana Mysuru
- Dr Rajesh, B.A.M.S.
- Raghavendra Raju, Kalari Sadhana Mysuru
- Drishith, Kalari Sadhana Mysuru
- Gunvith, Kalari Sadhana Mysuru
- Aadhya Arcot, Kalari Sadhana Mysuru
- Manu B, Photography
- Dr Shivaani Yadav G N, B.N.Y.S.
- Likith Yadav, M.Tech
- Sanjay V, Mysuru.
- Upasana Gurjer, Bengaluru
- Chandrashekhar (Nanjanagudu), Yuva Brigade.
- Mujeeb Rahman Pa Gurukkal, Lubaina Kalari, Ernakulam.
- Qurate Books Cover Design
- Aryan Singh, Publishing Manager, Qurate Books Pvt. Ltd. Mumbai
- Jonely Godinho, Book Designer, Qurate Books Pvt. Ltd. Goa

MY SOURCES OF KNOWLEDGE

krishnam vande jagadgurum

BIBLIOGRAPHY

- When the Body Becomes All Eyes. Paradigms, Discourses, and Practices of Power in Kalarippayattu, a South Indian martial art, Phillip B. Zarrilli
- Kalarippayat. The Structure and Essence of an Indian Martial Art, Dick H. Luijendijk
- Kalarippayattu: Guide Book, Jules Morel and Maneesh Mohanan
- Kalari Margam - Ancient secrets for modern living, Ranjan Mullaratt
- Kalarippayattu The Martial and healing art of Kerala, Shaji K John.

CONNECT WITH THE AUTHOR

Email: varungokulyadav@gmail.com

Website: https://kalarisadhana.com

Facebook: Kalari Sadhana :: Mysuru